Praise for
A Vision of Love

I0022469

"I warmly endorse Max Amichai's *Vision*, which touchingly reflects his love for the church to which I have given my life. He has experienced the best that true religious devotion can inspire—the gift of life in the face of devilish hatred. I have enjoyed sharing interfaith work with Amichai for more than a decade. His congregation Temple Adath Or and my Diocese of Mary, Mother of Hope in south-east Florida of the National Catholic Apostolic Church in the United States have worked together not only to appreciate each other's faith journey but also to improve life's journey on earth—notably with relief for my favorite group of loving orphans in Haiti."

—THE MOST REV. MICHEL JOSEPH PUGIN, O.S.B., PRIMATE
OF THE NATIONAL CATHOLIC APOSTOLIC CHURCH, MIAMI, FLORIDA

"The work that you have pursued is of enormous importance and your story is a powerful testimony of hope and perseverance."

—DR. CHRISTOPHER M. LEIGHTON, EXECUTIVE DIRECTOR,
INSTITUTE FOR CHRISTIAN AND JEWISH STUDIES

"In this evocative work, Max Amichai Heppner speaks movingly and powerfully from his heart to yours. Here you find a potent narrative of transformation. Travel with him as he describes his journey from a rather bitter Holocaust survivor to a broad-minded observer of the religious and social world, and onwards to embrace a compelling vision of compassion and love. You will be inspired."

—RABBI MARCIA PRAGER, DEAN & DIRECTOR OF THE ALEPH
ORDINATION PROGRAM AUTHOR OF *THE PATH OF BLESSINGS*

"In this book, Max Amichai Heppner unfolds his journey through fears and angers toward the vision he now holds of a world where Christians and Jews can embrace each other in loving and respectful ways. Through his captivating eyes, you may also come to appreciate what unites us all, rather than deplore what separates us."

—RABBI SHAFIR LOBB, PHD, RABBI, CONGREGATION EITZ CHAYIM, PORT SAINT LUCIE, FL, PROFESSOR OF WORLD RELIGIONS AND ETHICS AT INDIAN RIVER STATE COLLEGE, FORT PIERCE, FL, AUTHOR OF *BEDSIDE PRAYERS;* AND TWO SERIES OF PRAYER BOOKS: TO LIFE! AND TEFILAT HALEV (PRAYERS OF THE HEART).

I wholeheartedly support ecumenical dialog between Christians and Jews, and I admire Max Amichai Heppner's dedication to bringing Christians and Jews together.

FATHER JOSEPH TRAPP, PASTOR, ST. JOSEPH CATHOLIC CHURCH, PLAIN CITY, OHIO

A VISION of LOVE
for Christians & Jews

MAX AMICHAI HEPPNER

Published by:
Heppner Books
Hillsboro Beach, FL
www.heppnerbooks.com

Copyright © 2018 Max Amichai Heppner

ISBN: 978-0-692-44439-9

Cover and interior design by The Book Couple, Boca Raton, FL

All rights reserved. No part of this publication may be reproduced, scanned, uploaded, stored in a retrieval system, or transmitted, in any form or by any means, electronic, mechanical, photocopying, recording, or otherwise, without the prior written permission of the publisher.

Printed in the United States of America

A Call to Teamwork

"Coming together is a beginning.
Keeping together is progress.
Working together is success."

—SIGN IN THE BELLEVIEW BILTMORE HOTEL,
CLEARWATER, FLORIDA

To Hubertina (Dina) Janssen,
the mother who saved my life and
gave me the love of a Christian family.

To Rabbi Enoch (Hans) Kronheim,
who lovingly imbued me with the warmth
of Judaism and the love of Christians.

Contents

Foreword

A t the end of each chapter of this book, Max Amichai Heppner nails down another aspect of "his Vision of Love." I put "his" in quotation marks because I fully embraced his vision at the time it came to him, and I remember it clearly after at least two decades have passed. I can also feel some of the pain behind Max's vision. During our early conversations, I didn't get that so well, but after reading this book, I feel it deeply. In his book, Max Amichai shows why he is driven to setting relations between Christians and Jews on a new track.

Max is often deeply thoughtful, but early in our acquaintance, he was at one point surprisingly impulsive. We had just started working together as public information officers for the U.S. Department of Agriculture, headquartered in Washington, DC. We were riding in a Washington subway train, and, as we neared Catholic University, Max suddenly grabbed me by my elbow. He steered me to the door and popped me off the train when it halted. We were still miles from our intended destination.

Amazingly, Max had landed me at The Basilica of the National Shrine of the Immaculate Conception, which is also known as the National and Patronal Catholic Church of the United States. How could Max, the Jew, have known that I had wanted to see this site more than any in the capital city?

Wordless and wondrously, we walked into the cool interior. I knelt in prayer, and, to my surprise, I sensed Max kneeling beside me. Something striking happened at that moment. I was no longer with a stranger, someone I'd only met on the job a day or two ago.

I was with a Jew—and I knew in an instant that we were praying to the same God!

Our first moments at the Cathedral were already affecting me deeply. I had the feeling that God had put the likes of Max and me together for an experience that neither of us could ever fully understand, nor forget. Whether it was the magnificent edifice or a God who sometimes seems silent, sometimes ambiguous, is hard to say. Still, something suddenly inspired a unity of spirit between two people who hardly knew each other.

This sense increased when we went to the Chapel of Mary on the lower floor of the Shrine. First, Max started telling me about his childhood. This seemed unrelated to the occasion until he came to the part about how he had survived the Holocaust. It turned out he was saved by a family of Roman Catholics, who not only took him into their home but also into their hearts. And I thought, *Wow, now he is here in a holy edifice of Catholicism!*

It was then that Max had the vision that sparked this book and cemented our friendship. It immediately colored the whole experience of my visit to Washington, DC. We both felt the need to continue to pray together, and the manager of my hotel gave us the use of a conference room where we could do so in private.

If Max had been an Orthodox Jew, I might have felt awkward about relating so closely. Instead he struck me as a liberal, but reserved, European Jew. His build is slight, his vocabulary is expansive, and his voice is usually soft-spoken—to the point that I often have to strain to hear him.

In the days after our experience at the Cathedral, he started showing up at my hotel for prayer in a business suit with prayer shawl and kneeler in hand. At that point I knew for sure that he was no run-of-the-mill public servant.

Through Max, I gained a meaningful connection with his "people of the book." After I met him, my friend Myrtle and I were passing through the Jewish Quarter of Scottsdale, Arizona. By chance,

I glimpsed an English version of the Pentateuch (also known as the Torah, or The Five Books of Moses), and, on impulse, I bought it. When I began reading, I found much of the wording surprisingly "Christian." The ancient Jewish writers saw God as their "redeemer" and "salvation," concepts that Christians apply to Jesus Christ!

Understandably, my spiritual journey shifted; I became much more inclusive. It influenced me considerably once I became a board-certified chaplain, serving people of all religions. Max and I lost contact for a period of time, and we later resumed conversing through e-mails. These exchanges gave me a glimpse into his world, *par excellence.* Conversely, he saw my world more fully than he ever could have without our interaction.

There's no good reason why Jews and Christians cannot love and treasure one another. Christians believe that "God is love." Jews believe the same!

If you need convincing on this score, please read this book. It will expand your heart. Ask yourself, "Why should I limit love to just my own family, my own religious congregation or denomination? Why would we not want peace, justice, and equality to rule our hearts and guide our ways?"

A Vision of Love points to our best hope, not only for global survival, but also as the path to a joyous journey. My most fervent prayer these days is for a expansion of human consciousness so we can catch this vision and arise above former sentiments while growing more fully by knowing that God is a Lover! And the more we love, the more we are like our Creator.

—Joy L. Smith
Lake Havasu City, Arizona

Joy Smith publishes a website, Healing-with-Joy.com, which offers material for people of any faith orientation who desire to find emotional freedom and to grow spiritually. She is the author of *The Chaplain Is In: Journey to Health and Healing* and *Why Not Make the Trip Worthwhile?* Both are available at amazon.com.

Preface

My "Vision of Love" takes an unflinching look at how I function as an American Jew living in a basically Christian society. I examine the differences between our religious communities, and I share my belief that mutual understanding and appreciation can flourish despite these differences. My goal is to explore practical ways to promote mutual understanding and appreciation for Christians and Jews, and by extension, for all peoples who chafe under differences in their worldview.

I am motivated to tackle this topic because I was severely harmed by the nadir of tolerance in modern times, the Nazi persecution of Jews. In September of 1942, when I was eight years old, my parents and I narrowly escaped from the ghetto the Nazis created in Amsterdam in the Netherlands. We eventually found shelter on the farm of Harry Janssen and his family, who hid us in a chicken house for three years.

My book *I Live in a Chickenhouse* details our miraculous survival. It was first published in English by AuthorHouse Publishers, Bloomington, Indiana (1995 and 1997) and subsequently in Dutch by Ad Donker Publishers Rotterdam (2008), in German by MEDU Publishers, Frankfurt, DE (2010), and in Hebrew by the Yad Vashem Holocaust History Museum in Jerusalem (2016). It was expanded by a related video, "Rediscovering My Childhood" (1996) and a play, also called *I Live in a Chickenhouse* (2010). For details, see my website, www.heppnerbooks.com.

In writing the Chickenhouse story and presenting it to various audiences, I came face to face with a major question: *What's next?*

Do I reiterate the old story and keep pleading for understanding? Or do I go beyond that, and look for ways in which I myself can promote that understanding? Both paths seemed to have merit. The Chickenhouse series lets me travel along the first path. *A Vision of Love* takes me along the second path.

That second path involved a lengthy journey. My friend Chaplain Joy L. Smith, a leading advocate and student of Christianity, helped me along the way. We began modestly by coauthoring an article for a religious magazine and then continued thinking and writing on the same wavelength.

Joy and I met in 1989, when we worked together on public information to promote a grasshopper control program in Idaho, Montana, and North Dakota. We quickly realized our different strengths. I knew about the operations of our employer, the U.S. Department of Agriculture. Joy knew the mindset and needs of the ranchers involved. Never before had I been in close contact with a ranch-raised Westerner like Joy. On her part, Joy never had known a Holocaust survivor from Europe.

When our work together ended, Joy and I stayed in touch by cross-country correspondence and occasional visits. She helped shape my attitude toward and understanding of Christians and Christianity, and I hope I can lead other Jews to the same understanding. Naturally, I trust that Christians also will come to understand what troubles me about living in a society that they dominate. By getting to know my foibles and me, they'll better understand American Jews in general because they no doubt have similar problems.

Other people beside my friend Joy also are quoted in this book and helped me shape my ideas. I am deeply grateful to all, and yet I take full responsibility for everything I express in these pages.

—Max Amichai Heppner
Hillsboro Beach, Florida
May 27, 2018

1.
Seeing the Vision

I often recall a thought planted in my head by my teacher Rabbi Arthur Waskow when he discussed a central prayer of Jewish worship called the *Amidah*.

The prayer opens by calling on the divine as "the God of Abraham, the God of Isaac, and the God of Jacob," and Rabbi Waskow pointed out that the words "God of" are repeated but not redundant. Each Patriarch's vision is uniquely his own. So is yours; so is mine.

"That's okay," Rabbi Waskow said, "because the divine is broad enough to accommodate each person's individual conception. The Amidah is basically an invitation for a personal conversation with God."

So it doesn't worry me that my personal concept doesn't parallel that of the three patriarchs. I am much closer to the vision of a later biblical figure, the Prophet Jonah.

In the Book of Jonah, he frankly states that he wanted no part of the mission that God gave him: To prophesy to the citizens of Nineveh in ancient Babylonia. When God makes him undertake the mission anyhow, he considers it a fool's errand. In the end, he watches the outcome from a distance, feeling bitter and let down. In response, God doesn't give Jonah answers; God just makes him confront his own bitterness.

Sometimes I feel just like Jonah outside the gates of Nineveh. I want to sit in the shade of a carob tree and watch the craziness of the world from a distance. I want to get away from everybody and everything and sulk.

1

God rebuked Jonah for withdrawing and sulking. He said, "You're sulking under this tree that you didn't grow; I did. And you don't care about the big city, full of people who don't know their right hand from their left. I care for the masses, the animals, and the plants. Why don't you?" (My free translation: Jonah 4:10–11.)

Jonah didn't record his answer. I, as a follower of the God of Jonah, therefore have to find my own answer, my own meaning in life. I need to find a better way to face life than to feel bitter, complain, and withdraw.

For me, that isn't easy, because I am a Holocaust survivor. Like Jonah, I didn't want to go on a journey amid great dangers and among strange people. Hiding from the Nazis in a chicken house was for me no more comfortable than Jonah hiding from his mission in the belly of a big fish. As a result, I faced a searing question: "What is my life all about and why did it go so terribly wrong?"

Staring back at the question, I could see no point to it. My bitterness, like Jonah's, flavors to the question, "Why?"

Genesis of an Unusual Relationship

One summer day in 1989, the answer to that nagging question came to me, surprisingly in the form of a "vision." I'm not talking of vision in the sense of a "vision statement" like I prepared at work. I am referring to a vision in the sense of Fatima and Lourdes—a stunning supernatural experience. The vision occurred at the Shrine of the Immaculate Conception, the Mother Church of American Catholics, in Washington, DC, then just known as a Cathedral.

Before arriving at the Cathedral, my mind had been on the briefings I had prepared at the U.S. Department of Agriculture for Joy Smith, who had just come to work there. Our first stop was at the USDA's central office in Washington, DC. When our business there was over, Joy and I traveled on the Washington Metro to the suburb, where I worked in a satellite office.

As the train emerged from a tunnel, I spotted the Shrine out of the corner of my eye. My mind was idling, certainly not focused on religion. As the train rocked to its stop near the Shrine, suddenly, on impulse, I said, "Hey, Joy, you are a Roman Catholic, aren't you? You ought to see this Cathedral."

I pulled Joy to the door and pushed her out just before it slammed shut. She wondered what possessed me to do this impulsive act. And I wondered, too.

She collected herself quickly, and blinking at the departing train, she said, "Are you a mind reader or something? This Cathedral is the very place I most wanted to see when fate brought me to Washington."

"Must be thought transference," I said. "But strangely, I also love this place. This is an inspiring piece of architecture."

Once inside, I told Joy a more personal reason why this Cathedral attracts me. I explained that during the Holocaust, I had been saved from capture by the Nazis by the Janssens, a family of devoted Catholics, and the figurines at the Cathedral remind me of those that stood around their house.

Joy understood. We lapsed into silence.

An Apparition at the Cathedral

Then it happened. At one moment, my eyes were gently focused on the beautifully furnished altar of the Cathedral, and my feelings quieted. Then, suddenly, everything around me blurred, and the vision that inspired this book took its place.

I can't call it a revelation; it was more a feeling of being overpowered. To allow the vision to enter, my conscious mind was wrestled to the floor and pinned down.

I guess had to be immobilized because I am of a scientific bent, not a natural visionary. The experience was so otherworldly that I wanted to pinch myself to be sure I wasn't dreaming. I found I couldn't so much as blink my eyes, never mind pinching my skin.

The hair on the back of my head stiffened as my eyes locked onto the vision.

The figure of a man takes shape. He looks at me quietly. Benevolent, loving energy flows from him. His eyes are relaxed, as if he were waiting for the right moment to interact with me.

I tried to shake loose from the vision and reached out to Joy, but my voice was so hoarse, all I could do was croak out a single word: "Look!"

"What?" Joy answered. "Max, what do you see?"

I tried to clear my throat and rasped out: "See the man?"

"No, Max," Joy said again. "Where? What man?"

I tried to answer, but couldn't. I pointed above the altar.

I see the man, seemingly standing on something solid, but actually suspended in the air. He looks at us expectantly. His eyes look very kind.

Suddenly, I sense a message implanting itself in my head. I don't actually hear as much as a whisper; all I feel is a chill along my backbone. In utter silence, my every cell is taking in the message. It envelops and pervades me completely. It posits: "Love one another. Feel the love. Share it. You must establish love on earth."

Now my attention shifts to a visual message coming from the image above the altar. As I watch, the intricately embroidered border of the man's robe separates and arcs above him—starting at his feet, continuing around his head, and ending back at his feet on his other side.

A chain made up of the Hebrew letter Shinn shimmers in the embroidery and then starts dancing around the arc. The letters brim with energy. They stretch as if they are elastic. Then one Shinn snaps and the embroidery expands into a whole sentence: "Shema Yisrael, Adonai Elohenu, Adonai echad." It is the watchword of the Jewish faith: "Hear, O Israel, the Lord your God, the Lord is one." A hint of a smile on the man's lips seems to say, "You see, you also are all one. You need to find unity with each other."

I felt gagged. I tried again to see if Joy was seeing what I saw. Her eyes looked questioning, uncomprehending. For a moment, my awe at what I'd seen was tinged with irritation at her lack of reaction. Then I realized that, although the message seemed intended for both of us, I was the intermediary, not only to Joy but to everyone I could reach.

I can't find words to describe the urgency and insistence of the message. I can, however, tell you how it answered my gnawing questions as a follower of the God of Jonah. It meant, "Holocausts will continue to happen unless Jews and Christians employ the healing power of love. Both faith communities need to understand that we need to embrace each other with a love big enough to heal the pains of the past and to overcome the differences between us."

Comprehending and Sharing the Vision

I tried to convey the impact of my overwhelming experience to Joy the best I could. So I was bowled over when Joy responded, "Wasn't the man you saw the person of Jesus?"

Looking back at her reaction now, I realize I shouldn't have been surprised. However, at the time, my mind was focused on the idea imposed by the vision, by its imperative power. My vision wasn't about a "who"; it was about a "what." The "what" is a directive to wipe out the emotionally charged questions in our religions and instead focus on the love that religious institutions claim to promote.

If in fact it was Jesus who spoke to me, the message I heard was not to "come to Jesus" but to "listen to Jesus." His message was that if our two religious currents can't flow in the same channel, at least they can flow side by side without the one seeing the other as polluted waters.

Beyond that, the personage who spoke to me wanted us to help bring about the mission of peace, justice, and joy that the historical Jesus meant to bring two thousand years ago. My vision affirms that we are finally ready for this.

5

A Jewish Experience of Jesus

Today, I understand much more lucidly that Joy took my vision to mean that I had experienced a direct connection with Jesus. I couldn't follow her train of thought then, because it went along a track completely different from mine. I experienced the Vision as an appeal to promote love, not as a signal indicating I was ready to change my Jewish allegiance.

As I revision the experience today, I don't discount that Jesus may have appeared to me; after all, as a Jewish leader, he knew and performed Jewish prayers. I think he recognized me as a fellow Jew, and the encounter had no element of a call for me to convert.

I don't even consider it surprising that a Jew in a Christian environment encounters an experience of Jesus. Dr. Judith Orloff relates such an experience. In her case, it occurred in a nighttime dream when she was nine years old. There, her grandfather took her to a "larger-than-life" personage and specifically introduced him as Jesus. Inside the dream, she had no problem with this. She says, "I snuggled into [Jesus's] lap, protected and safe, lulled by a chorus of distant angels. At this moment, I felt only love." (From her biography, *Second Sight*, p. 166.)

Her mother cringed when young Judith recounted her dream. "Where did you get this from?" she challenged. "I've raised you to be a nice Jewish girl. We never taught you anything about Jesus."

Dr. Orloff reports that "throughout my childhood, [many dreams] communicated the same message of love, though with different characters and settings." These dreams helped her understand Jesus as messenger.

She concludes, "Years later, after a decade of meditating, searching, and studying with teachers from a variety of backgrounds, I [learned that] the bedrock of spirituality is to learn about love . . . . The form of spirituality is a matter of choice—it can be religious in a traditional sense, or not. After all, through the ages, spirit has had

6

numerous faces and names: God, Goddess, Jesus, Buddha, Adonai, Tao, Father Sky, Mother Earth, or love." (p.167.)

Dr. Orloff says that names don't matter. She holds that love incarnate can be any figure from any religion. I agree with her, but I don't feel satisfied. I don't live with just "any religion" around me. I live in a very dominant Christian environment against which I need to protect my Jewishness.

In other words, I still say "no" to a theological Jesus who died for my sins, even though I can embrace the Jesus of dreams. Jane Roberts, in her book *The Seth Material,* helped me understand that distinction.

Seth, her spiritual adviser, says (on page 188), "The Crucifixion . . . originated in the Universe of Dreams. It was a main contribution of that system to [our] own and could be physically compared to the emergence of a new planet within the physical universe." She explains, "Seth is not saying here that the Crucifixion was 'just a dream.' He is saying that though it did not occur historically, it did happen within another reality and emerged into history as an idea, rather than a physical event."

Another way of expressing that idea was suggested by the visionary psychiatrist Carl Jung, who speaks of archetypes. The impassioned story of Jesus's mission on earth is more fixed in the minds of millions of people than cold history or plain truth. It is a metaphor for the human condition, for the painful conundrum of a world supposedly striving for the good and failing in so many ways. It also stands for our eternal hope, expressed so well in the *Bhagavad Gita,* "God becomes man in order that man might become God." Jews and Christians can both sign onto these aspects of universal vision and achieve a true consensus.

Of course, it took weeks to digest my vision at the cathedral and begin to make sense of it—for myself, let alone for others. Right after I had the vision, I was dazed and confused. It was beyond me at that time to get Joy to understand the deep love that the vision wanted me to proclaim.

On that super-significant morning right after I had the Vision, the only words I could utter were evasive and prosaic. Lamely, I said: "If a saintly figure appears above a Catholic altar, you have to concede that it may be Jesus. Quickly changing the subject, I took Joy by the arm and added, "Come on, Joy, we have more people to meet." And I took her back to the Metro station.

In the days after the vision, I struggled even with myself to make sense out of it. Pointers from Caroline Myss, who, unlike me, is an experienced visionary, helped me out. In her recorded lecture "Energy Anatomy" (published by Sounds True Recordings, Boulder, Colorado), she emphasizes that the type of love I need to work with has to be unconditional. Myss says, "Unconditional love means the capacity to not have private agendas—to literally appreciate life enough so that the life force can run through you and be distributed to others. This is high-voltage energy. The universal teaching here is that love is divine power."

I connected with her words "high voltage energy" and "divine power" because that is what I experienced at the Cathedral. When ultimately I shared that insight with Joy, she understood that the vision was leading me not to Jesus, but to a deeper understanding of how a human society should function.

Visiting the Shrine with Joy became an event that changed both our lives. Our work relationship ended a few months later, but the powerful spiritual experience we had together generated a friendship that changed the way each of us looked at the world.

One of the first Jews with whom I shared my vision also surprised me with his reaction. "Visioning love," he said, "seems to be far closer to Christian religiosity than *Yiddishkeit.*"

Sure enough, the place where the vision overtook me is central to Catholicism—and if visioning love is a Christian approach, so be it. To me, the vision is a bridge, and a bridge can be crossed from either end. I am committed to constructing strong underpinnings for the bridge, and I hope others feel the same way.

However, even if we agree in principle, we still are left with finding ways to convert the principle into action. How we can actualize my Vision of Love is what we'll explore together in the rest of this book.

2.
The Challenge

Anger and resentment often get in the way when people try to actualize love. I know this first-hand. The fear I experienced from Nazi persecution and the anger it engendered still shadow me today.

Ironically, my pain about Germany and the Germans is worsened by my realization that, but for Hitler, I would have grown up in Germany myself. The imprint of Germany, stamped indelibly on the consciousness of my forefathers, was passed on to me in utero. I keep encountering it and feeling trapped by it.

For example, my ears instinctively perked up one day when, while I was eating lunch in a park near my workplace in Washington, DC, I heard tourists from Munich talking to each other. They were golden agers in the same age group as my mother, and their German sounded just like the way she talked.

My first impulse was to go over and say, "Imagine! You must be from Munich. Great! Munich is my mother's hometown. I am glad to see you. Enjoy your visit to beautiful Washington."

Before I could make a move or utter a sound, my feelings flopped. Now I wanted to go over and say, "Remember! Your hometown gave Hitler his start. Your German grates on my ears. Go to hell!"

My logical mind overrode both urges. It reminded me that Hitler is long gone, and I should leave these present-day Germans alone.

The truth is, I can decide to ignore present-day Germans, but I can't leave the past alone. It haunts me from the graves of my Jewish ancestors who lived in Germany for centuries.

For most of the 200 years since the Jewish Renaissance began, my forefathers tried to link their Judaism with German culture. They used every approach imaginable, and still they failed miserably. This unsuccessful effort is heart-wrenchingly detailed in Amos Elon's book *The Pity of It All* (Picador, 2002).

The book begins in 1743, relating the fierce determination of Moses Mendelssohn, a prodigy of Torah study, to take part in the dawning of Western culture in Germany, and ends in 1933, with the headlong flight from Berlin by Hannah Arendt, one of the last Jewish apologists for the German body politic. In between, I read the details of how fervently we German Jews loved our country and how miserably it repaid us. It sickened me.

We tried—ably, persistently, and nobly—to find a place under the umbrella of a united Germany, but German provincialism allied with a mythic feeling of Germanic superiority ruined it all. These proclivities held the non-Jewish German majority in such power that no civilizing effort could overcome them. Even though the German middle class became increasingly educated, they couldn't grasp the danger in their nationalism. Even when we Jews tried to join them in their nationalism, we were rejected.

I cried when I read Elon quoting Max Lieberman, who worked so hard for a rational German outcome after World War I. Just before his death, he said, "Regretfully, I have awakened from the beautiful dream of assimilation to a nightmare." When the Nazis later threatened Max Lieberman's widow with deportation, she committed suicide. She left a note saying she wanted "to be able to at least die here, in this city of Berlin."

The only way we Jews could unite with the rest of the Germans was to die with them! My own grandfather, Max Heppner, died in 1917 from the same heartbreak that felled Max Lieberman. We were overcome by our unrequited love of all things German.

Even at the time of Hitler's rise to power, some Jews bought new homes in Germany, thinking that non-Jewish Germans soon would come to their senses and rebel against the Nazis. The pity of it all is that this never happened. Elon thinks that a military coup in the early 1930s was in the air—but it didn't happen, engendering hopelessness in the Jews of Germany.

My family gave up on Germany at that time, the early 1930's. Had they remained, I would have been born in Berlin and would have spent my youth in the Tiergarten District where they and our many relatives were living.

Instead, my parents fled Germany in April of 1933 while my mother was pregnant with me. They came to the Netherlands, and so instead of me being born in Berlin, I saw my first light of day in Amsterdam.

Culturally, however I still grew up German. For example, let me relate how my family prepared and ate their breakfast eggs.

First, we punched a small hole in the air pocket at the round end to keep the shell from cracking while the eggs were being boiled. This operation was performed with an egg piercer, a cup with a small needle set on a tiny spring fixed at the bottom so that the egg would be punctured to just the right depth. When we were ready to put the eggs into boiling water, we upended a tiny hourglass, set to run out after precisely three and a half minutes. When the sand ran out, the eggs were quickly put into porcelain eggs cups and covered with woolen hats imported from Germany to keep them warm. We ate them with little German spoons made of bone to avoid the metallic taste of regular spoons.

Our conversation at breakfast was mostly in Dutch, but when it concerned those highly esteemed eggs, it was in German. The eggs were kept warm by *Eierhütchen,* spooned out by *Eier-löffelchen,* and lauded in terms of wonder, *"Ein Ei lässt sich nimmer erschöpfend leeren."* (Freely translated, this meant, "It's wonderfully difficult to scoop the last little bit out of an egg.")

I still eat eggs much like I did as a child. I don't use *Eierhütchen* any longer, but only a couple of weeks ago, I bought another

Eier-löffelchen. It really does keep the yolk from picking up a metallic taste.

Forgiving the Germans

In my family of origin, the German language was reserved for the grander things in my young life, and so the sound of it has always felt homey. Stacked against that is the sound of screams directed against us Jews by Nazis from Germany after they overran Holland in 1940. From table talk I heard since I was born, I learned to love German. From the invaders, I learned to hate it.

The paradox drove me crazy. In time, I realized that I had to separate the unremitting pain of the Holocaust from the resolvable anger at the Germans who had instigated it.

To start with, I decided to change my name. Up to that point, my name had been Max Bernard Heppner, which to me sounds totally German. Instead of changing it all, I focused on my middle name. Bernard is a variant of the German "Bernhardt," which means "heart of a bear." I dropped that, in favor of the Hebrew name Amichai, which means "my people live," a positive response to the Holocaust.

More far-reaching changes followed. I had long sworn that, after what the Nazis did, I would never, ever set foot on German soil. I saw all Germany as contaminated by bestiality.

That view changed when, during several trips to other areas in Western Europe, I gradually allowed myself to take notice of the Germans who crossed my path, and I saw that they behaved like human beings elsewhere. Beasts they weren't—horribly misled at one time, maybe, but still quite human.

I learned that, even in Berlin, a few non-Jewish Germans had helped Jews survive Nazi persecution. A study published in *Together* magazine (April 2008, page 7), conducted by the German Resistance Memorial Center, confirms that 1,700 Jews were successfully hidden in Berlin with the help of 20,000 involved non-Jews. I realized that human kindness had been present somewhere, even in the capital city of the Nazis.

Despite learning about Jews surviving with the help of non-Jewish residents of Berlin, I stayed conflicted about Germans and Germany. My feelings didn't soften much until I came across the conclusions of the Truth and Reconciliation Commission (TRC) of South Africa, another country that devoured its own inhabitants. The TRC cited "the monumental—some would say impossible—task of bringing together victims and perpetrators of apartheid-era abuses in a historic reckoning and healing process."

Anglican Archbishop Desmond Mpilo Tutu of South Africa eloquently explained the compassionate mindset behind this enormous task in an interview with Zia Jaffrey broadcast on television. In part of their conversation, Jaffrey asked:

> **Q:** Can you speak a little about the concept of *ubuntu?*
>
> **A:** *Ubuntu* comes from the root [of a Zulu-Xhosa word], which means the essence of being a person. You can't be a solitary human being. It's all linked. We have this communal sense, and because of this deep sense of community, the harmony of the group is a prime attribute.
>
> Anything that undermines the harmony is to be avoided as much as possible. And anger and jealousy and revenge are particularly corrosive, so you try and do everything to try and enhance the humanity of the other, because in that process, you enhance your own, since you are bound up with each other.

I came to better understand this concept in 1994 when I had to go to Berlin on business. I used my free time there to walk through malls, parks, and street fairs—ordinary city venues. And the people I saw were ordinary city people. Not monsters, just *ubuntu,* "persons."

It took time for that understanding to sink in. I was greatly helped by my cousin Peter Paetzold, whose parents succeeded in disguising their Jewish background during the Holocaust and never left Germany. In 2003, I contacted Peter and asked him to help me introduce and reconnect me to the Germany I had missed.

He and his wife, Gisela, lovingly took me in, along with my then-wife, Shana, and daughter, Liora. Together, we visited kind friends, old churches, new synagogues, and the graves of our relatives. In the process, Germany came to rejoin the human race and I rejoined my German past.

So how do I cope now with my memories of the Holocaust? I just posit that the Holocaust happened because it happened. The Germans were the way they were because they were the way they were.

When people hear me tell the story of how I survived Nazi persecution during the Holocaust, they sometimes ask, "Do you feel lucky to have survived?"

I haven't been sure how to answer. I do feel lucky, but that feeling is offset by survivor guilt. After all, Michael Graumann, my companion while we were on the run, was murdered virtually in front of my eyes. By contrast, I survived multiple dangers without even a physical scratch.

I discovered reasoning that made the most sense to me in a column *Ask Marilyn,* that had a long run in *Parade Magazine.* The columnist, Marilyn Vos Savant, was billed as the smartest person on record per her top score on an IQ test. I'll summarize her reasoning; I can't quote you the whole column because I have lost the clipping and don't remember the date of publication.

Marilyn postulates two accidents. *In one scene, a victim is struck by a car while walking on the sidewalk; in the other scene, he is struck while walking in the street.*

Marilyn explains that the victim walking in traffic was in the wrong place at the wrong time; the one on the sidewalk was in the right place at the wrong time—just like me. I was just a school kid minding my business when the Nazis kicked me out of school and then threatened me with deportation to death camps.

So does Marilyn's reasoning let me forgive and forget? No. I still feel the pain in remembrance, and I struggle with forgiveness.

I also talk about it a lot. For example, it came up in a conversation I had in 1995 with Dr. Richard Johnson, a lecturer in the human potential movement. He knew before we talked that I was a Holocaust survivor. We didn't pursue that topic immediately, but apparently his mind was working on it while we were talking.

Eventually, he asked, "As a Holocaust survivor, how do you handle your feelings towards the Germans? More than six million murders seem like an unforgivable offense."

As soon as he asked, my mind started racing. *Should I reveal my inner struggle to this relative stranger?* I decided to go ahead.

"The Holocaust has become a metaphor for unspeakable evil," I began. "The numbers involved seem too great to get our minds around. Once you try anyhow, you see that the forgiveness dynamic doesn't get more formidable along with the enormity of the transgression. Is it more acceptable to commit one murder than ten? Is ten more okay than a hundred, a million, six million? It's humanly impossible to decide at what point to draw the line between forgivable and unforgivable murder."

That was pretty theoretical. When I started feeling a bit more at ease, I reached deeper into my feelings.

"Forgiveness really does not rest on impersonal numbers," I said then. "It is tied to intimate and personal events—from the horror of my grandfather's murder down to the loss of my first bike, which the Nazis confiscated in front of my face early during their persecution of Jews in Holland."

"Still, you're faced with huge numbers," Richard said. "You must see guilt in the entire nation of Germany, am I right?"

"You're right," I replied.

Undeniably, I used to hate all Germans, and I didn't realize how much it cost me to be a hater until my anger boiled over. The time was the summer of 1979. The place was a beach in Zandvoort, near Amsterdam, in 1979.

I sat looking out at the ocean, and suddenly I felt the anger eating away at my guts. I visualized ripping the anger out of myself and drowning it in the ocean.

Of course, that didn't work existentially, but it indicated that if I didn't get relief my guts would erode incrementally. Finally I achieved the resolution I wanted in a dream.

My rabbi and I are going down a river in an amphibious jeep. Suddenly, we see a snake uncoiling out of the water. I am petrified because its mouth spits and its awful fangs snarl millimeters close to my face.

I turn to my rabbi and say, "Help! How do I get this awful snake away from me?"

The rabbi answers, "Just talk to it. You know what to do."

So I say, "Snake, you scare me. Please back off and go away."

To my surprise, the snake backs off and recoils into the waters.

The rabbi in the dream is Marc Labowitz, who leads a Monday class focused on achieving our human potential through the teachings of Judaism. Imagine my surprise when, the following Monday, I saw Rabbi Marc actually standing next to an image of the snake from my dream. It was painted into the fresco of our classroom. I hadn't consciously noticed it before. It was part of a large, complex design, but apparently my subconscious had picked it up.

It didn't take me long to figure out what the snake is trying to say, namely that it is time to face and defuse my old anger. I now understand that since I give that snake its power, I also can take it away.

I also realize that the snake isn't my enemy, but actually a potential protector. When I feel anger arising in me, I ask the snake to help me direct my life toward the "yes in the world," the way Rabbi Marc describes seeing the world through more positive eyes.

Still I feel a dissonance. I can get the "yes," but I still couldn't get the "why" that came up in my talk with Dr. Johnson: "But why condone murder?"

Anita Epstein, a fellow member of a support group called "Child Survivors of the Holocaust," critically examined this question in an opinion piece published in the June 9, 2010, issue of the *Jewish Daily Forward*. The article, titled "Why I Cannot Forgive Germany," wades right into the topic, saying:

> The overwhelming majority of today's Germans obviously were born after the Holocaust. Do they nonetheless share guilt for the actions (or inactions) of their parents and grandparents?
>
> I myself could not forgive today's Germans. It does not trouble me that contemporary Germans live with the hurt from that past as well. After all, just as children inherit wealth and otherwise benefit from what their parents achieve, so do they sometimes inherit their parents' debts, including this one.
>
> I am unpersuaded by those who favor forgiveness because the act often makes the person doing the forgiving feel better. I have long felt tolerably well about myself. The idea of forgiving those who perpetrated the Holocaust would have the opposite effect: It would make it hard for me to live with myself, to get out of bed and look in the mirror. I could not dishonor the memory of my family members and the millions of other Holocaust victims by giving a free pass to their murderers.
>
> For sins against others, Jewish law and tradition require offenders to express remorse, genuinely repent, provide recompense to victims if appropriate—and directly ask the victim, three times, for forgiveness. [Criminals like] Josef Mengele did not repent, and he did not beg victims for forgiveness. [No one alive has] the power to forgive Mengele, so far as Judaism is concerned.

I follow Anita's reasoning and connect with her feelings. However, I didn't feel "tolerably well" about myself when I kept stewing about what the Germans did.

I never had a chance to thrash out the differences in our thinking with Anita, but I had a closely related, quite revealing conversation with another woman. She approached me for no apparent reason to complain about the pain, anger, and unforgiveness in her heart.

This woman's way of going on about her feelings made me think in terminology I learned in Transactional Analysis: *This woman wears a message on the back of her T-shirt that says, "Kick me." And she finds plenty of people in her environment to comply with her "kick me" message.*

I imagine that the message Anita wears on her own T-shirt is: *Pity me. I'm a Holocaust Survivor.* That message, I think, is self-destructive.

To parallel the relevant sentence in Anita's article, I'd say: *It would be hard for me to get out of bed and feel good about looking into the mirror if I kept on agonizing about burdensome memories of the Holocaust.*

I honor my murdered family members and the millions of other Holocaust victims not by unforgiveness, but by seeking conciliation with the Germans of today. Of course, I recognize what Anita calls the inherited burdens of *contemporary Germans [who] live with the hurt from that past."* Our difference stems from my not wanting to live in the past except through forgiveness. Forgiveness is important work, and to function at its best, the world must heal even the deepest, most hurtful wounds.

When Anita's reasoning goes along the track that *for sins against others, Jewish law and tradition require offenders to express remorse,* she refers to a familiar Jewish religious ruling. It's a healthy ruling, but I believe she misapplies it. It refers to everyday spats between living people who share the same community, not a murderer and his victim, totally unrelated and both dead. It is the living to whom we owe extending forgiveness or at least understanding and a hand offered in hopes of creating a more loving world.

So I am firm in my stance that differs from that of Anita and many other survivors who feel like she does. I look for reconciliation, yet I realize that I still resent the Universe for using a Holocaust to teach me to live my life in love.

I brought that issue to Dr. Dorothy Mihalyfi, who offered me the opportunity to explore it through past-life regression. Under her guidance, I left my current life and let myself wander through time to a previous life that related to my question. Another version of myself appears in a trance:

I am an Eskimo fisherman named Amik, age twenty-four. There's an endless world of ice and snow all around me, an expanse so vast that it makes me feel small and bewildered.

I hear Dorothy's voice, "How did you die, Amik?"

In response, the trance changes.

I am standing on a block of ice, trying to snag a fish through a hole in the ice. One of the members of my tribe sneaks up behind me and pushes me into the icy water. I go under, wondering why, when all of us in the tribe so much depend on one another, this fellow wants to kill me. I drown, not knowing the answer.

When I told Dorothy about my trance experience, I added: "So what do I learn from that? How am I better off now?"

And she replied, "Well, look, Amichai. This time you came out of the experience alive."

Somehow, I could connect with the karma. However, I couldn't grasp the connection between the action of a single, irrational member of a primitive Eskimo tribe and the actions of millions of Germans who enthusiastically supported the Holocaust. How could a people steeped in Western culture and science have perpetrated such a horror?

The best answer I have found appeared on the Internet in 2006 as part of a discussion on "why this world is controlled by a terrorist minority." My most vivid attention was drawn to a post by Paul E. Marek of Saskatoon, Canada, entitled, "Why The Peaceful Majority Is Irrelevant." (Paul is a second-generation Jewish Canadian immigrant, whose grandparents fled Czechoslovakia just prior to the Nazi takeover.)

In his post, he quoted an unnamed member of the pre-Nazi German aristocracy, who supposedly once owned a number of large factories and estates. Whether real or imaginary, Marek posted a conversation with this anonymous aristocrat:

Marek: How many German people would you say were true Nazis?

Aristocrat: Very few people were true Nazis, but many enjoyed the return of German pride, and many more were too busy to care. I was one of those who thought the Nazis were just a bunch of fools. So, the majority just sat back and let it all happen. Then, before we knew it, they owned us, we had lost control, and the end of the world had come. My family lost everything. I ended up in a concentration camp and the Allies destroyed my factories.

Marek: (Interrupting this dialog): We are told again and again by 'experts' and 'talking heads' that . . . the vast majority [of any human society] just want to live in peace. Although this unqualified assertion may be true, it is entirely irrelevant.

It is meaningless fluff, meant to make us feel better, and meant to somehow diminish the specter of fanatics rampaging across the globe. It is the fanatics who march, who . . . wage shooting wars worldwide, who systematically slaughter [various] groups, who . . . bomb, behead, murder, or honor-kill. The hard, quantifiable fact is that the 'peaceful majority,' the 'silent majority,' is cowed and extraneous.

A supporting view of how the Nazis "hijacked the morality of ordinary Germans" is propounded by my friend Fred Katz, himself a child survivor of the Holocaust. (See his book *Ordinary People and Extraordinary Evil: A Report on the Beguilings of Evil*, published by State University of New York Press, July 1993.)

Fred sees standard Western morality as a bundle of beliefs, including, perhaps, "the rights of man," "the nobility of patriotism," and "the need to love your neighbor." So Fred concludes:

> Ordinary Western people can do Holocausts when one of the beliefs in their moral bundle becomes paramount. Say, for example, that you are a breadwinner who's out of work and you're offered a job if you join the Nazi party.
>
> You accept the bait on the very moral motto of 'Support Your Family.' As this belief in supporting your family becomes preeminent, you let 'Love Your Neighbor' and all the other beliefs in your moral bundle fade into insignificance. If the Nazis help you support your family, nothing else they do can seem bad.

When I mentioned Fred's theory to Dr. Richard Johnson, during the conversation that I cited earlier, he said, "That theory fits right in with a personality test I'm developing. I'm trying to measure people's capacity to employ a moral trait like 'Love Your Neighbor.' As I work, I'm discovering to my chagrin that a person capable of loving his neighbor is equally capable of hating his neighbor. In other words, the ability to express any trait can work negatively as well as positively."

"That's scary," I replied, "and it sounds just like what occurred with the Germans. What scares me the most is that if we don't watch out, it can occur with anybody!"

"Yes, it's scary," Richard affirmed. "Any great lover can easily become a champion hater."

The positive side of this is that a hater, like me, also can become a champion lover. Each of us, I've come to understand, must be a careful guardian of love. If we want to realize my Vision of Love, we must not let the love-hate pendulum rebound toward hate if things don't go right in our lives.

This conclusion directly affects my internal arguments of how I should view today's Germans. This came up graphically when my wife and I went to Berlin again in 2010. In that environment, I had a dream.

A friend and I are cleaning up trash left over after an art workshop. The trashcan is full, and we try to stuff down the junk. However, there is no room for it all, so we let it pile up behind the trashcan. Under a pile of trash, we find artwork we did during the workshop. My art is hidden in a thick folder, but my friend's work is painted on the inside of cookie can lids. His subjects all are scenes of ordinary people happily having a good time together.

The dream tells me again that I can't get far by wallowing in the trash of life. It emphasizes that if I look beyond the trash, at how people can live lovingly and supportively together, then I can rediscover the beauty of life and love.

Ram Dass expressed it well in his book, *How Can I Help* (Alfred A. Knopf publishers, 1986, p. 177–178), "The only way to achieve [reconciliation] . . . is to remember, again and again, who we all are behind our terrible conflicts. . . . We may be humans with deep differences, but we are all humans, all God's children. . . . And that vision [of unity] must be profound and all-inclusive, an affirmation of heart and soul. It must be strong enough to stay alive, often under the worst of conditions."

Stacked against that realization, I am faced with digesting the horrors perpetrated by Germans because, willy-nilly, I keep hearing them retold by survivors, in person or via memoirs they share with me. Irresistibly, the old anger resurfaces.

I interrupted my writing at this point to study the Torah segment for the week, called *Ki Teitzei* "When You Go," which contains a directive from God [Deuteronomy 25:19], that seems self-contradictory. It says, "When the LORD your God gives you rest from all your enemies . . . you shall blot out the memory of *Amalek* from under heaven. Do not forget!"

Many readers, including me, ask themselves, *How can you remember to forget?*

All of a sudden, I intuited that I'm already doing the reverse of what *Ki Teitzei* requires, which is just as impossible: *I'm trying to forget to remember.* Therein lies the answer to dealing with my feelings that still rise up when recalling the Holocaust.

Matched up with my dream about cleaning up trash after an art workshop, *Ki Teitzei* tells me: *What you remember about trash— about the Holocaust—is on the outside. Don't look at the dirty outside of the cookie tin, look at the art hidden inside the lid. In other words, look inside your own heart and soul. That's where you will see beauty and find release.*

Forgiving the Enmity of Christians

Even if I am more at peace with the Germans for their role in the Holocaust, I still have work left in forgiving Christians. That goes especially for the Roman Catholic Church, whose preachments of hate for us Jews spanned nearly two millennia.

The Office of the Inquisition stands out as a horrid example of a church-sponsored organization supporting hate. It arose in Italy in the thirteenth century and gained its major expression and notoriety during the reign of King Ferdinand and Queen Isabella of Spain (1479 to 1516). It even spread throughout the vast Spanish Empire in America along with the conquistadors. It lasted in Mexico until 1820 and in Europe until 1834, meaning that its last victim died during the lifetime of my great-grandfather.

The physical presence of the Office of the Inquisition can be felt even today. Its headquarters building in Mexico City still stands. Part of it is set up as a museum exhibiting the instruments of torture used by the Catholic authorities to extract confessions from their Jewish and other assorted victims. The Congregation for the Doctrine of the Faith, the successor agency to the Office of the Inquisition, is still an arm of the Roman Catholic Church, headquartered at the Vatican in Rome.

The Inquisition, even though the Church instituted it, was morally bankrupt. It was used as a blatant scheme for Christians to enrich themselves at the cost of Jews. The customary reward for betraying Jews to the Inquisition was a gift of property belonging to the betrayed. Influential businessmen used the Inquisition to eliminate Jewish competitors in their field.

Let me cite a particularly horrid example, the case of Don Luis de Carabajal (or Carvajal), one-time Governor of the Mexican State of Nuevo Leon. He acquired considerable land holdings from the Spanish Crown in return for settling and pacifying the region.

Lesser notables, with an eye on Don Luis's properties, denounced him and his family to the Inquisition in 1590 for "Judaizing." All Jews who lived under the governance of the Spanish crown were forced to convert to Catholicism, but many secretly maintained some (or many) Jewish practices. This "crime" was dubbed "Judaizing."

All members of the Carvajal family were tortured to secure a confession. Artists of the time showed the wife of Don Luis stripped naked and flayed in front of her supposed equals among the landed gentry.

The "gentry" achieved their goals. After the entire family was executed by burning at the stake in 1595, the accusers were able to take over the valuable lands that Don Luis had been granted by the Crown.

The Church instigated the Inquisition, and it also played a role in supporting the Holocaust, although its involvement isn't as clear-cut. Dr. David I. Kertzer, a Brown University historian, examined the Church's support of the Nazis. He published his conclusions in *The Popes Against the Jews: The Vatican's Role in the Rise of Anti-Semitism* (published by Alfred A. Knopf, 2001). He concluded that, for most of a century and a half leading to the rise of Hitler, the Catholic Church not only turned a blind eye toward anti-Semitism, but "actively, knowingly, purposely contributed to it, lending it authority and respectability while honoring the most active purveyors of this vicious series of canards against the Jews."

To save their positions or their skin or to just get along, European Catholic and Protestant leaders bowed to the Nazi regime. Priests and Nazis acted in unison in performing a "Heil Hitler" salute, as recorded in *Comparative Histories, Christians and Jews in WWII Europe* by Dr. Miranda Pollard, Professor of History at the University of Georgia.

With notable exceptions, church leaders at best sat on their hands while the Holocaust took place under their noses. There was no will to act. Those religious figures who did help the Jews were principally on the lowest rungs of the church hierarchy, acting on their own.

Jews had it better in America, but don't think anti-Semitism "only" existed in Europe. In the 1940s, American voices spouted the same canards and hate-lust voiced by anti-Semites in Europe. They were led by a Roman Catholic priest known as Father Cochran, who gained wide notoriety through his radio broadcasts.

Anti-Semitism in America didn't disappear after the Holocaust. A nationwide survey of two thousand people released by the Anti-Defamation League late in 2007 showed 15 percent of the respondents had intense anti-Semitic sentiments, which the League said was the first increase in overall anti-Semitism in over a decade.

That's statistics. Let me also cite a personal example: For our honeymoon in 1958, my newlywed wife and I had tickets of admission to a tennis club in Virginia Beach, Virginia, as part of our vacation package. However, when we appeared at the club's gate, they turned us away, saying, "We don't allow no Jews."

When we returned home, I complained to the travel agent who had sold us the vacation package. The agent shrugged it off. "If you want to avoid that sort of thing," she said, "book your vacations with the rest of the Jews in the Catskills."

I realize, of course, that today my life isn't threatened. Many Christians in my life are supportive friends who have no problem with my being Jewish. Nonetheless, the fire of my paranoia is still refueled constantly. It comes from demeaning Internet blogs (which I can avoid); from newspaper articles (which are harder to ignore); and even from gratuitous comments by reporters with a national reputation, such as Helen Thomas, the first female president of the White House Correspondents' Association.

On May 27, 2010, Thomas told Rabbi David Nesenoff, who was at the White House for a Jewish Heritage Celebration, that Israeli Jews should "get the hell out of Palestine" and "go home" to Germany, Poland, and America. That resulted in a wave of denunciations and a measly apology.

Actually, Thomas's hatred of Jews had been documented many times before. For example, during a 2004 speech to the Al-Hewar Center, a Washington-based Arab organization, Thomas likened Palestinian protesters resisting the "tyrannical occupation" by Israel to "those who resisted the Nazi occupation." You can well imagine how her suggestions that Jews should "go home to Germany" and that Israelis "act like Nazis" stung me personally.

Less irritating personally, but equally telling, are examinations of America's big three newspapers, *The New York Times, The Washington Post,* and *The Los Angeles Times.* For example, according to the Spring 2008 issue of *Media Report,* all three of these national newspapers ran long columns by Arab officials damning Jews, while printing exactly zero articles by Israeli officials. There wasn't even a modicum of balance during the nineteen months of the study that spanned part of 2006 and 2007.

The *Media Report* added that *"The New York Times'* outgoing bureau chief Steven Erlanger continues to romanticize Palestinians in quasi-poetic style, suppressing key (unflattering) facts about their media, mosques, schools, and politics that engender hatred and violence and block reconciliation with a Jewish state."

The supposedly liberal national media aren't even balanced by the supposedly right-leaning small-town press. My teacher, Rabbi David Zaslow, who lives in Ashland, Oregon, the population of which is less than 22,000, sent me several juicy pieces from his hometown newspaper. One that particularly cut into my flesh as a Holocaust survivor concludes, "The victims who moved to Israel [from Europe after surviving the Holocaust] have shown they are no better than the victimizers they fled."

In an America that I share with segregated tennis courts and biting attacks in the newspapers, it is tough to reach out to Christians. In a way, my anger at Christians is as complex as my anger at the Nazis. In each case, I share their culture while at the same time I experience their dislike at my being a part of it. I have to work hard to overcome my discomfort about that.

This feeling is reflected in a ditty I learned from one of my coworkers at the U.S. Department of Agriculture, my employer for most of my career. He was one of the few rare Jewish birds in that aviary. The ditty goes:

Roses are reddish, violets are bluish
If it wasn't for Jesus
We'd all be Jewish

Being Jewish, we take the world more seriously. My Jewish coworker engaged me about collecting funds for Israel and about honesty in the workplace. Another close coworker, who was

Protestant, seemed so much more at ease. He liked to talk about ways to handle a big rock in his lawn and about decoding vanity license plates. In comparing the conversations of these two, I feel that a Christian's life fits so much more easily into his surroundings.

This feeling was reflected in one of my dreams, which featured these two coworkers.

The two of them are having a fight in my Jewish coworker's house. They throw hammers with sharp claws at each other. Each throw misses, and instead of hurting my two coworkers, the hammer claws tear at the walls and woodwork in the house. I sense they are destroying the house.

I freeze with fear, as I usually do when there is violence and conflict around me. When I can move again, I walk into the next room and pack my treasures. They are all bits of jewelry made by children, like an armband of beads and a lapel pin made from a decorated safety pin. I realize that I've stored this jewelry in a separate room since childhood.

The dream reveals that deep inside me, Judaism and Christianity have a terrible time living together. Their discord tears up the fabric of our society and threatens my survival. Furthermore, the treasures in Judaism that I esteem are trivialized.

The difficulty I have in sharing these treasures showed up in another dream:

I am leaving my place of work, but I can't get past the guards because I only have a temporary identification card. The only way I can get out is to squeeze through a narrow tube like the one they use for an MRI. When I get out at the other end, my parents are waiting for me in their car. They tell me about two rabbis who are coming to town.

The dream emphasizes that I find it oh so difficult to connect the passage leading out from the Christian environment at work to the religion and culture of my parents and rabbis.

The dream asks the question I'm exploring with you: Why am I a Jew adrift in a Christian world? Wouldn't it be so much nicer if there hadn't been a Jesus, and we all were Jewish?

For years, I have focused on what Christians can do to make this a better world for Jews. In the end, I realized that the direction of my thinking needs to change. I told myself, *It's not just about them; it's also about me. I can't ask Christians to change unless I, myself, am willing to change.*

I tried to ignore this imperative, but it pursued me. It grabbed me by the collar, of all places, during a course in Supervisory Training held at Western Maryland College in Westminster. After a tiring day of classes, I had already gone to sleep when I was awakened by some fellow conferees. I got up to see what was going on.

Some rowdy but good-natured conferees were play-acting some imaginary scene. The best I could tell, imaginary knights were parading toward some imaginary castle with an imaginary Cinderella in tow. Cinderella was dressed in white flowing robes; I could tell who she was because they had lettered "Cinderella" on poster paper and pinned it on her back.

I checked to see where they had gotten their poster paper, and I found a stack of it in a conference room. Sleepily I thought, *We all ought to pin a sheet on our backs, like that Cinderella girl. So identified, we could explore openly what role we are playing in the world.*

Next, I felt an impulse to pin a role on myself. I grabbed a sheet, wrote the first word that came to my mind, and taped the paper to my back. It said "The Truth." Immediately, I had a chance to test out that role with some other conferees who were leaving a late-night gab session in the lounge.

"I am The Truth," I said jokingly to a good-looking woman. "Would you like to embrace The Truth? The Truth is The Word, and if you embrace it, it will set you free."

The woman laughed and gave me a playful hug. The hug felt warm and good, but I felt uneasy. Something was wrong with my act. My sleepy head had come up with a phrase that parodies beliefs about Jesus. This phrase must surely have deep meaning for Christians, but what did it mean for me? What is my own Truth that could set me free?

Then the Truth hit me so eerily that it raised the hair on the back of my neck: The truth that I needed to embrace was Forgiveness and the people that I had to forgive were the Christians in my world.

Real forgiveness is serious work, beyond mere words. Many people who say they've forgiven still have daydreams of revenge. To quote Caroline Myss again, "You may forgive a person in your head but until it's in your heart, you're fooling yourself. Your head may say a hundred times, 'I have forgiven.' But unless your heart is aligned with your head, you'd still offer your mother's right arm to see the supposedly forgiven party twist slowly, excruciatingly in the wind."

I keep working on the issue of forgiveness. Another dream I had underscores this:

I am walking down a street in the winter. It is cold. Puddles on the sidewalk are frozen into thin layers of ice, and people walking there are slipping and sliding. I come to a fence with a small, towel-like rag draped over the top. It seems alive, and when I tug on it, it snaps back.

The dream showed me that I was still on slippery ground. I needed to get off the fence with regard to forgiveness, lest I snap back into anger, which hurts me double.

A Jewish teaching says, "Who takes vengeance or bears a grudge acts like one who, having cut one hand while handling a knife, avenges himself by stabbing the other hand." (Jerusalem Talmud, Nedarim 9.) I saw that, in order to deal effectively with my underlying anger, I need to accept Christians as fully human, and I need to be open for them to project their beliefs on me.

I was fortunate to have my friend Joy to help me with that. She had lived a life quite different from but just as complex as mine. Neither of us took in our faith "with our mother's milk." We came to our faith through decades of effort. The path to faith presents some formidable obstacles to the seeker, as I discover in pursuing my Vision of Love.

3.
The Path to Faith

In the course of our discussions, Joy and I decided to review our individual paths to faith. We wanted to clarify our position for ourselves and to come to a deeper mutual understanding. We had to fully embrace our own religious faith and comprehend that of the other to reach the level of reconciliation needed to realize my Vision of Love. As my teacher Rabbi David Zaslow once put it, "You have to descend into particulars before you can rise back up to the level of Universalism."

Amichai's Journey

To summarize my own path, I like to quote a poem that Rabbi Zaslow taught me, composed by an earlier wise teacher, who lived in Spain from 1092 to 1167.

I Rouse My Slumbering Thoughts
by Rabbi Moses Ibn Ezra

My intellect beholds visions from the Almighty
And I understand that the Lord is within me;
That his precious Self is hidden,
But His works reveal Him to the eye of thought.
He kindled a lamp, lit with His glory, in my body;
It shows me the ways of the ancient sages.
And this is the light that grew brighter in youth
And shines even more, now that I am old.

Following "the light that grew brighter in youth" was a challenging journey. I feel its shine more intensely only "now that I am old."

The Lord's "precious, hidden self" stayed hidden for me as a young child because the works of the Lord did not reveal Him to the "eye of thought" in my parents. They both were basically agnostics.

I was never able to explore my father's beliefs, adult to adult, because I was only eleven when he died. However, he imparted his critical view of organized religion with a song he liked to sing with me. In Dutch, it's called, *"De koekoek en de ezel."* In English, that would be "The Cuckoo and the Donkey," and the lyrics would sound something like this:

The Cuckoo and the Donkey
The cuckoo and the donkey
Set up to compete
In musical ability
With songs that sounded neat.

The cuckoo said, "I beat you,"
But sounded like a crow.
"Oh, no, I am the champion,"
The donkey brayed out so:

"Cuckoo, cuckoo,"
"Ee-aw, Ee-aw,"
"Cuckoo, cuckoo,"
"Ee-aw, Ee-aw."

It's a kiddie song, but along with the silly lyrics, I think Father wanted to say something like this, "Man has created God in his image out of fear of the unknown. A fearless, open-minded man in a free society has no need for such a primitive and superstitious concept. God as an explanation of a quixotic world may have made sense to our nonscientific forefathers. But a man of erudition and science is beyond such concepts."

Father was happy and secure in his self-concept as *Herr Professor Doktor of Philosophie.* For him, life started at birth and ended at death. In his view, it is up to the person walking that path to make the most out of it, using his brain, his brawn, and his beneficent attitude toward his fellow man, especially to folks lacking Father's own highbrow erudition.

In terms of family history, few families I know are as far removed as mine from the God of our Fathers. My father's father also was an agnostic, and my great-grandfather, though more steeped in tradition, didn't seem to have disabused either of them of their unbelief.

In the history of man, three generations of agnosticism doesn't seem a long time. The combined lifetimes of my father and his father and grandfather don't quite cover a century. But in the history of a family, where memory generally stops at stories passed on from great-grandfather, a century is a long time. Unbelief is part of my inherited family history.

Father wasn't arrogant about being agnostic. One of his friends in Amsterdam, Max Wolf, was a true and sincere believer, and Father respected Max absolutely. Father, Mother, and I celebrated the Passover Seder every year with Max and his warm, extensive family. It was the only religious observance we attended, and to Father, it wasn't a spiritual experience; he enjoyed it as a folk custom.

His calling a Seder a "folk custom" wasn't snobbery. In fact, Father cared sincerely about Jewish folk customs and the Jews who followed those customs. In Germany and Holland, where he lived, Jewish institutions are supported by means of a voluntary "religion tax" collected and then distributed by the government. Father annually registered himself as Jewish on his tax return and cheerfully paid the extra tax.

Father valued his Jewish heritage and expected me to do the same. As soon as I entered public school, he arranged for Max Wolf's son, Moses, to teach me Jewish history, Jewish law, the Hebrew language, and other non-devotional aspects of our culture.

My mother's father, Jacob Kramer, lived with my parents and me when I was young, and he alone seemed to grow somewhat closer to God as he matured. In his late sixties, Grandfather started going to the *Lekstraat* synagogue in my neighborhood, and occasionally, as part of his childcare duties, he took me along. But he never imparted any religious content to me. I accompanied him to synagogue and waited while he prayed in the same way that I accompanied him to his interminable card-playing sessions and waited while he played pinochle. I understood no more about religion than I did about pinochle.

While religious practice remained foreign to me, Jewish lore remained in front of my eyes. The last school that the Nazis permitted me to attend was a Jewish summer school that followed first grade. I still can sing the Jewish songs I learned there in 1941.

When deportations of Jews in Holland began in 1942, my family and I went into hiding. As good fortune would have it, a rabbinical student was in hiding near us. He was Rabbi Jacob Soetendorp, who reestablished the Liberal Jewish community of the Netherlands after the defeat of the Nazis. For many months, he conveyed lessons from his hiding place to mine. Father added them to my homeschooling, but he treated them with no more veneration than reading, writing, and arithmetic.

Despite his scientific, non-emotional stance, Father never discouraged me from praying. Where I picked up the idea, I don't know. It may have been principally from my Catholic foster parents, the couple who supplied us our hiding place.

My foster mother was a true believer. She took her children to Mass each Sunday and sent them to parochial school. They all studied their catechism, and I copied them.

The birthday presents I received from my foster brothers and sisters were "trading cards" of saints and holy men and women. It may not be kosher, but I have an affinity for these saints. When I lose something, I still call upon Saint Anthony, and he consistently has helped me. So that is the religious environment in which I started praying.

When we fled from Amsterdam, I was concerned because we had to leave my grandfather behind. I asked God to protect Opa at his Jewish old-age home so he'd be there for me after Liberation.

It was not to be. We heard from an eyewitness that the residents in his old-age home were all deported to Nazi extermination camps. Opa survived the awful journey in a cattle car, despite his weak physical condition. He was murdered with poison gas in 1943 at Sobibor in Poland.

In pain and grief upon hearing this, I read God out of my life. I thought, *Perhaps Father was right saying that God didn't exist. Else, perhaps He didn't care to hear my prayer.* I felt abandoned and angry. I had asked God only one favor in my entire life, and still He had failed to deliver.

After Liberation finally came, we were contacted by Jewish organizations in the West who were searching ravaged Europe for surviving Jewish children. They arranged with the military authorities to have a Purim party for the ones they had found. One fine spring afternoon in 1945, they sent a U.S. Army truck to pick me up. It was the only army truck ever to have come down our dirt lane. I felt very special!

I expected they would be giving us a party. I was bewildered when instead they had us sit down on benches to listen to prayers led by an English Army chaplain. Yes, I suppose I had experienced that sort of thing passively when Opa had taken me to synagogue when I was little. Now the soldiers gave me a booklet with Hebrew and English prayers, and I was supposed to be saying them.

I wasn't fluent in either language, so I just leafed through the booklet and waited for the party to start. I think I understood that Purim commemorated a plot to murder all Jews in a far-away country, but I doubt I was able to make a parallel with the Holocaust. The prayers did intrigue me, but there was no follow-up.

My father died soon after. After his death, my uncle Frans, a friend of his, undertook my tutelage. If Father had been agnostic, his friend Frans went him one better; he was an outspoken atheist. If I so much as mentioned God, I got a stern lecture!

My mother took me to the United States after my thirteenth birthday, and we moved in with Mother's sister Helen and her husband, Max Forchheimer. Uncle Max had been raised Orthodox with a solid religious schooling, and he remained a practicing Jew.

Uncle Max wasn't pushy with his religion. He held a service at home every week to welcome the Sabbath, and I accepted that as part of the many strange things I encountered in a new country.

However, I was taken aback when Uncle Max started a new ritual with me every Saturday morning. He would pat me on the shoulder and say, "Listen, young man. I am going to Temple. Will you come along?"

I didn't know what a Temple was and didn't ask. I just shook my head no. Uncle Max would give me another little pat and say, "Very well, I will go by myself." He put on his hat, picked up a little blue bag holding his prayer shawl, and walked out the door.

Uncle Max had few other conversations with me. He worked into the night six days every week, fully absorbed in his work. So after several weeks of his asking me to go to "Temple" on Saturday and my saying no, I relented. I wanted private time with him, and I wanted to see where this hardworking man went on his day off.

His "Temple" turned out to be an unused party room above the Tasty Shop, an antiquated deli in an aging Jewish neighborhood. The place was dark, poorly ventilated, and unadorned, but a faithful group of elderly German Jewish emigrants gathered there every Saturday morning. The service was in Hebrew, of which I understood practically nothing. The sermon was in German, of which I understood the words but not the meaning.

Yet I still learned something important in that dank Temple full of refugees. They called their organization "The Gates of Hope," and they obviously made it a portal into a new life and a new country. The procedure wasn't orderly—quite un-Germanic—but it had a definite form and a beauty of its own. Going there several Sabbaths in a row bonded me with my uncle and with his old friends; it gave me a warm feeling of belonging.

Then Uncle Max popped an even more surprising question. "Max," he said one day as we were walking to his Temple, "you are thirteen. It is high time you became Bar Mitzvah."

And so I landed in the Gates of Hope Sunday School on weekends and in its Rabbi's apartment on Thursdays after school to prepare for Bar Mitzvah.

Lovingly, Rabbi Enoch Kronheim taught me from the many books of Jewish lore that lined his bookshelves. He was close to seventy years old at the time, but he was as enthusiastic about learning as if he were an eager boy of seven. His soft fingertips caressed the pages of the Torah, and his lilting, somewhat hoarse voice patiently sang and re-sang the trop, the melody of the recited Bible that I was supposed to learn.

I became Bar Mitzvah on the wings of the Rabbi's generosity. I hardly understood any Torah, but in the process of trying, I came to understand something more personal and revealing. I got it, that the only reason the Nazis put so much effort into trying to kill me was that I belonged to a group of people with a special way of relating to God. I realized that the Nazis hated hallowed Jewish texts and burned them when they could. They despised prayer, abhorred the feasts of the Jewish calendar, and ridiculed Jewish foods and customs.

If that was so, I thought, *by God, I am going to practice these very things they hate.* I wanted to clearly show they hadn't stopped me.

I attended Hebrew high school, and I continued reconnecting with my Jewish heritage when I went to college at the Ohio State University in Columbus. I was an active member of the Hillel

Foundation, the Jewish community's outreach to students. In fact, I found that I had absorbed enough prayers at the Gates of Hope to do a good job of leading them for Hillel.

Despite my involvement with religion, I couldn't feel a strong spiritual connection. I still felt like Jonah, who recognized God but didn't have a good relationship with God. So I also looked outside of Jewish practice. I explored spiritualism and worshipped for a time with a group of Spiritualists. I then looked into Indian lore and joined the Self-Realization Fellowship of Paramahansa Yogananda.

I think I developed most through my work with a study group sponsored by the Association for Research and Enlightenment, a branch of the Edgar Cayce Foundation. Our text was called *A Search for God,* and we explored the nature of the divine—and what belief in the divine demanded of us. I learned that I could come closer to God by becoming a more rounded and more involved person.

More recently, I have become on more intimate terms with God through the message and practice of Jewish Renewal. I completed the two-semester Core Group Program of the Jewish Renewal Life Center in 1998, and I have been an enthusiastic supporter and student of this "phenomenon," as my teacher Rabbi Marcia Prager has called it.

She explained, in personal correspondence dated February 9, 2006, "Jewish Renewal is not a formal denomination with a formal hierarchy or structure. It is the ongoing creative project of a generation of Jews who are seeking to renew Judaism and bring its spiritual and ethical vitality into our lives. At the same time, it embraces a global vision of the role of all human beings and spiritual paths in the transformation of life on this precious planet."

Earlier, I had learned of the spirit world "out there," as taught by spiritualism. In Jewish Renewal, I discovered the spirit "in here." I found exactly in what way I am made in God's image: in spirit. Spiritually, I now am reconciled with God. Maybe I'm ready now to tackle my Vision of Love.

Joy's Path

Here's how Joy described her path to faith:

During my early childhood, my family did not attend church, and talk of God was excluded from our home. Yet, for some reason, Mom and Dad sent me to a Quaker girls' camp when I was eight years old.

During the first evening service there, Jesus Christ was introduced in such a loving, caring way that my heart was deeply touched. The building where we met was called The Tabernacle. It was made of actual logs. The floor was deep, soft sawdust. I can recall that rich smell even now!

At the end of that first service, campers who wanted to accept Jesus into their hearts and lives were invited to validate their decision. Immediately, I felt called to come forward to kneel at the altar rail. As I walked along the sawdust-covered aisle, I could easily feel and internalize the love and appreciation for this Jesus that the service leader had so aptly portrayed.

Every night for the rest of the week of camp, I walked down that "sawdust trail." I smile while thinking of how greatly I must have wanted to make sure my acceptance "took." Yet I think those multiple trips to the altar were more and more about wanting to experience that new love of Jesus.

When I came home, my parents began attending church with my sister and me, and perhaps my camp experience had a lot to do with that. Years later, Mom and Dad became ministers, and they started traveling to numerous countries to expand Christ's teachings. What an outstanding change had taken place in our family! My parents had two more children, and today, each one of us is doing some sort of ministry with people in need.

The decision I made as an eight-year-old was the most significant event of my life. God seemed very near to me throughout my childhood and early teens. Throughout life, I have continued to place the Gospel of Jesus above all other readings.

I had knowledge only of Protestant churches until 1976, at age forty. However, I was disturbed by the great number of denominations within Christianity between which so little unity existed. To recover some of the unity and solidarity in Christianity, I began studying the teachings of the Roman Catholic Church.

I expanded on that base by taking instruction from Father Andy Schumacher in the late 1970s. He and other teachers in the Church portrayed God's love and goodness, and I came to trust more fully in the acceptance and mercy of God. I gained a sense of how we are to be with others in ways that bless them and help them to know they are loved. To a large degree, those teachings also spoke to my quest into meditative and contemplative prayer. Four years later, I formally joined the Church.

Even so, I had been opening to Roman Catholicism while struggling with life-threatening illnesses that plagued me between the ages of thirteen and thirty-five. I don't know why I had to be sick for so long, with a tendency to form blood clots that traveled to my heart, then landed in my lungs.

At any rate, while I was hospitalized at age thirteen, I had a loving introduction to Catholicism through the Sisters of the Holy Cross who were chaplains who tended to the spiritual care of the patients. They imprinted upon me the power of a listening, loving presence. I came to know that illnesses, losses, and trauma do not have to be negative experiences. I saw that God was not angry with me or punishing me and that suffering has a redemptive side. I was not a failure, or less than, because of being sick. Instead, the nuns taught, God was right there with me in the midst of my struggles. Ever since, I have gained much from wrestling with these "interferences" within life.

After twenty-three years of practicing Catholicism, however, I found that I no longer could embrace some of the Church's ancient tenets, especially the notion that we are to seek suffering in order to be holy. Time brought further shocks when the sexual abuses in the Church came to the surface in 2002. What pained and repulsed me most were the devious methods used by the bishops to hide and protect sex offenders. The very leadership that I and other church members had trusted had proved to care more about the reputation of the Church, with its practice of secrecy, than it cared about the safety of children.

No longer could I stay within that framework, and my studies at the time also prompted me to further examine my theology. So, my path made a switchback to the Protestant arena of Christianity, specifically the Presbyterian Church USA. Thankfully, I now see more efforts among Protestant denominations toward reaching a greater level of unity.

My husband, Gary, and I chose membership in Presbyterian churches, and in time, I became ordained as a deacon by my congregation. We like how accepting this group of Christians is toward various other beliefs. We also appreciate the many avenues the Church pursues for serving the requirements of the members, the needs of our city's poor, and broader global concerns. Within that denomination, I also could maintain my interest in interfaith activities. Universality is essential to me, and my association with Max has reinforced that stance.

I have found a keen satisfaction in being with people in such a way that prompts the love of Christ to surge up from within. That is true, no matter what the background of these people might be. I minister because I love God and I love people.

The illnesses I suffered taught me compassion. This led me to begin my initial studies and training toward working with sick and dying people in hospital, hospice, and jail settings. Once I received degrees in psychology and theology and became a board-certified chaplain, I could more effectively help people who struggle with matters of the heart. As a mental-health provider, I could also serve those suffering from emotional and mental torments. I was a Roman Catholic layperson when I was board certified by the National

Association of Catholic Chaplains. However, I had a long wait before I could satisfy my wish to become a certified professional. I couldn't start the training until our three sons were raised. Then, I had the time and the opportunity to do the work of my heart.

Even though at that time I was a practicing Presbyterian, I found this mode of service to be genuinely fulfilling. It fit the model of serving "the Christ in others" that the Sisters of the Holy Cross had modeled for me.

I also found that a spiritual director can greatly assist people's personal growth, and I had my own spiritual director for thirty years. So I decided to enter a two-year training program to become a spiritual director. I followed that training by completing my master's degree.

My education was finished at age sixty, after which I opened my private practice in mental-health counseling and spiritual direction. Serving at our local hospital has been part of my life throughout at least two decades. Each aspect of my profession involves listening, being a sounding board for people, and granting them the opportunity to advance in their journey as they learn to hear and to follow God.

As I serve, I learn that I receive back in the same measure as I give. I have grown, and I know that we all can learn to find our own answers. We do that by learning to "trust" and to listen to 1) the prompting of God's voice spoken within, 2) how God speaks through others, 3) how God speaks through life's circumstances, and 4) how God speaks through nature. Through these learning experiences comes innate strength, emotional healing, and emotional freedom.

Today, my health is good. My recovery from serious illness was an answer to prayer. However, it took place slowly through a practice of journaling, meditation, and contemplative prayer, which brought a better understanding of myself and of God's call. Certainly, my recovery correlated with learning how to identify my feelings and to deal with them honestly. I learned to practice acceptance and forgiveness of self and others. This brought me growth in the areas of self-esteem and the ability to love others.

The most significant personhood I've encountered, of course, is that of Jesus Christ, whose life and teachings I continue to ponder and attempt to live out. For that reason, I consider my conversion to Christianity at age eight to be the most significant event of my life. It allowed God's merciful love and grace to be evident and has challenged me to seek to understand God and to grow in wisdom. I experience God's presence through meditation, journaling, and prayer, as well as by observing nature, the gifts of daily life found through others and through reading scripture.

My practice has healed me in many ways. All I know is when my soul healed, my body followed suit and my health has become better than most people's.

Through the decades of my life, God's mercy and grace have become ever more evident. My goal is to stay on the path of seeking God's will over my own, day by day. Mentors and teachers sent by God helped me stay on that path and inspired me to thirst for more and more knowledge about God.

There still are gaps in the faith into which I am growing; imperfections keep popping up. As a believer, however, I seek my remedies by staying in service. I try to extend to others the kind of love I've experienced from God and from others whose lives portray God's nature. I am gently called back from straying, whether from noxious pastures of bitterness, hate, lack of forgiveness, or revenge. All these are forms of selfishness that lead to self-destruction and pain for myself and others.

What many people call prayer, I call "being with Him," calmly contemplating the wonders of "Presence." What can I say of all those intimate moments I've spent with Jesus, whom I know as Lord? My experience of Jesus bonded me to God, whom Jesus called "Father." Ultimately, I came to know that God has characteristics of both "father" and "mother." I no longer have problems with that language.

Further, I have in Jesus an ongoing advocate who pleads my case before the Father. Out of love and devotion to God, I continually seek to sense the wonder of having been forgiven—and so I have learned to forgive others.

As a Christian, I have experienced the reality of God through Christ, and I believe the Father and the Son and the Holy Spirit are One God. This is a mystery in which we Christians place our trust. It is not at all unusual for a Christian to say that the Lord has spoken to him. Hearing the Voice of Christ within me over and over again throughout many years makes me sure of it. This voice is ever calling me back into the love, forgiveness, and humility that it takes to have patience. Through what is often called the "mystical experience of God," I have encountered the Spirit of Jesus Christ alive within me.

The fruit of a thing proves its worth. Since that fateful day at summer girls' camp, I have experienced the reality of God. I have experienced day-by-day providential touches of love that are simply unexplainable. Living at that level surely removes all barriers between Jews and Christians—and anyone else. It certainly has led me to a kind of spiritual awareness akin to what Max calls the "Vision of Love."

4.
Repeating the Vision

J oy and I corresponded for years about our faiths, and I think
I used that exploration to avoid the mandate that came with
my vision at the Cathedral. Another vivid experience with Joy,
about seven years later, gave me a strong reminder to implement
the mandate.

At that time, in 1995, I was visiting Joy and Gary at their home
in Lake Havasu City, Arizona. We did fun things together, like
cruising in their ski boat under old London Bridge, which the town's
developer, Robert McCulloch, moved from its site in England just
for the publicity it generated. (He even created a waterway for the
bridge to cross by cutting through a peninsula on Lake Havasu.)
We did other touristy things that I'll skip over to come to the con-
sequential event on the Sunday morning when Joy invited me to go
to Mass with her.

We arrived early at Joy's little white parish church, but the priest
already was at the door. I was introduced as a Jewish friend; the
priest was introduced as Father Rudy. He smiled kindly.

We then entered the portal, passed the font with holy water,
proceeded down an aisle, and settled into a pew. The organist was
playing a few introductory hymns. We listened with equanimity
until, bam, there came my message through a totally unintended
happenstance.

In his introductory recital, the organist started playing what
probably started as a Croatian folk melody and was later arranged as
a hymn by Franz Joseph Haydn in 1797. In the hymnal, it is titled

46

"Austria" or "Austrian Hymn," but it is better known by its opening line, "Glorious Things of Thee Are Spoken." The lyrics are based on Psalm 87:3, and I later found them on the web in a version by John Newton (Olney Hymns, London: W. Oliver, 1779), as follows:

Austrian Hymn

Glorious things of thee are spoken,
Zion, city of our God!
He, whose Word cannot be broken,
Formed thee for His own abode.
On the Rock of Ages founded,
What can shake thy sure repose?
With salvation's walls surrounded,
Thou may'st smile at all thy foes.

A Reminder

Of course, the organ music in Joy's church was wordless, and I didn't know the lyrics of the hymn.

However, the lyrics to that melody that I *did* know seriously alarmed me; they were the words to the Nazi National Anthem, *"Deutschland, Deutschland Über Alles"* ("Germany Reigns Supreme"). As soon as the first chords reached my ears, I felt my heart shift into panic mode.

Easy, heart, I said to myself. *They're not playing that song. It must be an old Christian hymn that the Nazis appropriated. Look! No one else that's come to Mass seems alarmed by this hymn.*

That realization reassured my heart, but my mind raced backward through my history. I thought, *What if I was a Jewish kid pretending to be Christian during the Holocaust? What if the organ in my foster mother's church had played the Nazi anthem? Could I have stood it? Would I have given it all away by screaming and running from the church?*

As if to provide an answer, I was thrown into a time warp. My mind's eye shifted to another scene, although current reality peeked through as the scene unfolded. Inside the time warp, it wasn't 1995 any longer; it was 1942.

Suddenly, I am no longer a sixty-one-year-old man invited to a Mass by a friend; instead, I am eight, and my foster mother in Holland is taking me to church for the first time. I am frightened to the edge of panic because I have to pretend I belong there. I have to behave as if I really were Catholic like everybody else.

Could I pull it off?

Greet the priest outside, on the steps? I could do that. "Good morning, Father." Lovely man. He smiled at me with a most loving look on his face.

Urn with holy water inside the portal? I could handle that; just do as Mom does. Just plain water. Doesn't burn.

Kneel in the pew when you get there? Doesn't hurt; the kneeler is padded. You can pray quietly; you don't have to know anything.

Suddenly the organ strikes up the music to "Deutschland Über Alles."

What!? Will they sing that? Must I also sing that? Is it a trick, to find Jews in church? No, relax, it's organ music, it's just organ music, and they're not singing to it. It's an old Catholic hymn, very likely. These people around us, they're all friends of Mom's. They aren't out to hurt me.

But do they know I'm Jewish? Never mind. Pay attention. They're crossing themselves. Concentrate.

Oh, I learned to do that. Forehead before chest, left breast before right breast. Mumble about the Father, the Son, and the Holy Ghost. Amen. That's easy.

They're singing now. It's another hymn. I'll fake it. I can sight-read along or, if necessary, just move my mouth as if I'm singing. I can respond to blessings, respond to prayers, even pray in Latin! Mom, did you know that Jews can learn Latin? What? Be quiet, don't talk about

Jews? Of course not, Mom, I was just whispering. I'm nervous, don't you know? Oh, God, what now? It's time for Communion. Do I go up there with the others?

Joy rose to take part in Communion, and I blindly followed her in the delusion that she was my Mom and I needed to do what she does.

Confused about what was happening, Joy whispered into Father Rudy's ear.

I made out her words: "Father, can Max take Communion?"

"No," I heard him answer. "That's not authorized. Not unless he's baptized."

Slipping back into my time warp, I thought: *What? Does this man want to baptize me? He wants to change me. So I won't be me?*

The priest smiled at me again. That calmed me down some.

In my time warp, I quickly assessed the situation: *Yes, he's a lovely man. He won't hurt me. He knows I'm just adopted. He won't make me be baptized.*

And my mom, what does she want me to do?

That new question was so shearing that it cut me out of the time warp, and it pierced the veil through which I had been glimpsing the present. I again saw myself as a grownup and realized I might have caused a scene during Communion.

I was back in 1995, but the fear from 1942 stayed with me. I wondered, *What would it take for me to be accepted by this Catholic community here in Arizona? What if they knew I was Jewish?*

In the midst of this agitation, another vision imprinted itself on me, as if to give me the answer.

Suddenly, the countenance of Father Rudy officiating at the altar starts taking on an ethereal look. His body emanates force fields of pure love—broad sheaves of pulsing energy—which flare up from the altar every time he approaches it. The force fields in the altar abate when Father Rudy moves away, but they never die out. They flare up again when he comes closer. They are so bright as to be blinding.

I became aware that I was again flipping out because I felt a trickle of tears dripping from my eyes. My body was responding to the blinding light that only I could see.

I suddenly felt a great sadness. I once again felt I would never be able to truly describe the power of the love that I experienced at the Basilica in Washington. If I couldn't even describe it, how could I harness it?

Underneath the sadness, however, I started to notice a reassuring foundation of confidence. I realized that the very power in the light could and should be transforming. The light of love had to be the bridge that spans the difficult gap between Christianity and Judaism.

The vision in the parish church and the internal conversation about it busied my mind. I was out of touch with the outer world until I heard someone whispering in my ear. It was Joy, and she was even more agitated than before. She wanted to tell me that the service was over, but I slipped into the time warp again.

What, Mom? Oh? Stop daydreaming? Time to shake hands with the folks in the pew behind, in the pew in front? I can do that!

Mechanically, I turned around, stuck out my hand to the man on the seat behind me, and said, "God be with you, my neighbor."

I heard him echo back, "And with you, my neighbor."

The voice inside me continued, *Would you still bless me, my neighbor, if you knew I was Jewish? Would you turn me in?*

No, stop, I said almost aloud. *Let go of that time warp!*

I managed to pull myself together, but the experience stayed in my consciousness.

It's hard to put such a vivid experience into words. Some groundbreaking psychologists, Dachel Keltner and Jonathan Haidt, tried it in, of all venues, a scholarly article ("Approaching Awe," *Journal of Theoretical and Philosophical Psychology* 22 [2002]). They say:

> Some experiences are so vast, so profound,
> so far beyond what we have previously perceived,
> that they in effect demand that we transform our
> world view in order to accommodate them.
> This may explain why some . . . experiences have
> the potential to be life changing.

My experience during Mass changed my life exactly in that way, and it returned me to reconnect fully and actively with my mission to actualize my Vision of Love.

Putting Your Life on the Line for a Jew

I liked the experience of the repeat vision, suggesting, as it did, what it takes to inspire rescuers to help Jews in trouble: Dina Janssen's big, open heart provided the answer, and I heard it echoed by another rescue story from that era. It is an amazing big-hearted action from another daring, inventive, self-motivating Dutchman, named Jan Zwartendijk.

By coincidence, I heard his story directly from two personal sources: One, his daughter-in-law, was a high school friend of mine; the other, Jan's biographer, was a cousin of mine. From them, I learned that Jan was as little prepared for the role of rescuer as my foster mother when fate offered him an opportunity for action and he responded instinctively out of a pure sense of love.

Jan worked as a sales rep for the Dutch electronics firm Philips Gloeilampen, and in a bureaucratic shuffle in 1939, he was appointed regional sales manager for Lithuania. Like many multinational firms, Philips carried on its business oblivious of politics and wars, but Jan's reassignment pulled him straight into political troubles stirred up by the Nazis.

Just after Jan's appointment, Germany provoked World War II by invading Poland, a country bordering Lithuania, and panicking German Jews who had fled to Poland now were streaming into Lithuania. I suppose that Jan Zwartendijk was only vaguely aware of this refugee problem, and he became involved in it only through a highly unusual circumstance. It turned out that the current Dutch consul in Lithuania alarmed the Dutch government by his strong pro-Nazi leanings, and they recalled him to Holland.

The now-vacant consular position proved hard to fill—the winds of war made it difficult to send a professional diplomat from Holland, and the Government, hearing about a Dutchman on site, asked Jan Zwartendijk to act as an interim consul. On impulse, Jan accepted.

In his new role as Dutch consul, he was approached by a Dutch-Jewish woman who found herself trapped in Lithuania by the sudden declaration of war and the German take-over of Poland. The woman told Jan that she wanted to return home to Holland, but she feared traveling west through a war zone.

Instead, she considered traveling to Holland by going East, meaning leaving Lithuania, traveling across Russia to Japan and from there across the Pacific to the Americas. There she would go to Curacao, a Dutch island colony off the coast of Venezuela, from where there still was commercial traffic across the Atlantic back to Holland. She asked Jan whether even with her Dutch passport she would need a visa to enter Curacao and whether he could arrange transit visas for the countries she wanted to cross on her eastward journey.

Jan consulted the diplomatic precedents, found no reference to visa requirements for Curacao, but for safety's sake, he devised a Curacao visa and put it in the lady's Dutch passport. He then contacted diplomatic colleagues from Russia and Japan, and they agreed to issue her the necessary transit visas.

Somehow the desperate German-Jewish refugee community

in Lithuania heard about the Dutch woman's travel arrangements. They came to Jan and asked whether he could issue them visas for travel to Curacao as well, even though they had German passports.

Seeing how desperate the German Jewish refugees were, Jan went ahead and issued Curacao visas for them on his own initiative. Then he again approached the diplomats from Russia and Japan to see whether they would support the refugees wanting cross their countries. Together, the three diplomats agreed to set up a procedure that supported international travel from Europe through Asia and onto Curacao in the Americas.

As soon as the option out of Lithuania became known, Jan was besieged by applications from trapped German Jews. In response, Jan stopped all work for Philips, and instead set up an assembly line to process visas. He worked so efficiently that the Russians and Japanese asked him to slow down, as they couldn't keep up with their end of the paperwork. However, they all did their best. Jan believed that, like himself, the other two consuls truly wanted to help the refugees.

In a matter of less than two weeks, until the Soviet government closed that escape route, 2,200 Jews made their way East on Jan's Curacao visas. Few, if any, actually reached Curacao. About half found ways to get to the Americas, Israel, and other "safe" countries. The Japanese rounded up the rest and interned them in Shanghai, where my cousin Ernest got to know many of them personally. (Ernest had landed in Shanghai via another last-minute escape route from Germany.)

Ernest said Jan Zwartendijk was motivated by true human decency, the same impulse that I call love—the kind of love also shown by my foster mother. However, I still wanted to know whether other rescuers had different motivations. The famous motion picture *Schindler's List* tells the shady side of the story. Oskar Schindler was no humanitarian; he saved Jews by the hundreds because they were cheap labor.

Young Jewish children like myself didn't necessarily encounter human kindness as a motivation for the rescuers. The case of Mania Weinzweig illustrates that in a heartrending way. Her story was published in *Mishpocha,* the newsletter of the Federation of Jewish Child Survivors.

Mania was just eight months old when the Nazis invaded Poland. Her parents feared for her safety and took her to live in a convent in Klimintov. The nuns accepted her and kept her alive, but barely so. And they exacted a terrible price when her father frantically came looking for her after he survived the horrors of Auschwitz and Buchenwald. Mania spelled out the details:

> When I was found, I had a head full of lice and was very bloated due to malnutrition. I hated Jews; they killed Christ, I was taught. . . . The convent would not give me up. They lined up all the little girls facing the wall, and [my father] had to recognize me from the back. . . . [Then they] demanded 5000 Zlotys for [me]. . . [I have] a letter that my father wrote . . . to the Kielce Province Jewish Committee . . . pleading with them for the money for the redemption of his daughter. . . . [After I left,] I felt that possibly I was an impostor and the real Mania was still in the convent.

Clearly, the answer in Poland was that very few people put their lives on the line for a Jew. And among those who did, many people wanted far more than the biblical fifty pieces of silver for one little life, like the "Women of God" who took in Mania.

I am deeply grateful that, for me, it was different. Still, I wondered about the neighbors. If I had landed in the next house, would I also have been saved with care and love?

I found a relevant answer in an article by my friend, Ed van de Kerkhof, a journalist writing for the Eindhoven's *Dagblad,* the regional newspaper for the area where I was hidden. The article, part of a series called "War and Remembrance," included interviews with a cross section of people in the region.

Their responses showed that, before the Nazi persecution, most interviewees didn't know any Jews; at best they knew them as stereotypes. They spoke of "calf Jews" who showed up periodically to buy up surplus cattle. Later, when Jews came running to the area to escape the Holocaust, they weren't received with open arms. We city Jews looked even stranger to the locals than the former "calf Jews."

"No Jew counted for much anywhere," said a farmer from Deurne in a quote from the survey. "Even so," he said, "you couldn't just stand by and have them be ground to pieces."

That particular farmer didn't just stand by. He is Frans Goossens, who sheltered and saved several Jews. When Ed, the journalist, tried to interview Frans about his motives, he said, "I never spoke about this during the war, and I kept my mouth shut after the war. So why should I talk about it with you now?"

So why did Frans take the actions he did? Ed answers, "Out of a stubborn conviction that his view of the world mattered more than the view of the authorities. He did it because he thought it was the right thing to do."

However, in fact, most neighbors did close their eyes when we Jews were being "ground to pieces." Ed says that most people also closed their ears. When the fact came out that nearly 90 percent of the Jews in Holland had been murdered, the rest of the populace didn't want to face that they had done nothing to help. People like my foster parents and Frans Goossens were given medals and recognition by the State of Israel and Jewish organizations, but hardly a word was said about it locally in Deurne.

When Ed published his "War and Remembrance" series, one article, headlined "The Forgotten Grave," raised a lot of commotion and involved me personally. The grave in question, located in the Protestant cemetery in Deurne, held the body of a young man called Michael who had been murdered during the Nazi occupation.

When the murder occurred, Michael and his parents, Heinz and Elli Graumann, had been on the run from the Nazis, together with me and my own family. The people who were supposedly helping us escape had suddenly decided to kill us, but had succeeded only in murdering Michael.

My journalist friend Ed discovered that the people of Deurne had forgotten the gruesome murder. In fact, caretakers of the local Protestant cemetery were about to remove Michael's grave to beautify the cemetery.

When Michael's surviving relatives and I heard about this, we petitioned the town fathers to keep the grave intact. In the changed climate of opinion, they responded positively and even designated his plot as a "Jewish cemetery," arguably the smallest Jewish cemetery in the Netherlands.

Altogether, Ed's article achieved the shocked reaction he strove for, and people in Deurne finally started dealing with the forgotten story of Jews who had come to the area for rescue. When the Day of Remembrance for which Ed had written his series finally arrived, this change was evident. The mayor, the priest, and a representative of the queen spoke of the place we hidden Jews have in the history of Deurne. That made a big difference for me. I was present for the observation, and that day, I no longer was just a vague shadow there.

I don't know if the people at the ceremony saw beyond my slim figure on stage with the town leaders. Did they also think about my nagging question, "What does it take for a Christian to put his or her life on the line for a Jew?" I really don't know.

I can tell you, however, that it meant a lot to me to see my foster mother Dina Janssen finally get the local recognition she deserved, even though she was nearly ninety years old by that time. I realized that putting your life on the line for another human being requires a dose of love in your heart large enough to overshadow personal risk and public opinion. That love can be accessed by anyone and is a key ingredient of my Vision of Love.

The Drag of the Diaspora

Some people have called any Jew of the Diaspora a *Wandering Jew.*
This image, or archetype, comes from thirteenth century Christian
legends about a Jew who taunted Jesus on the way to the cross.
For that sacrilege, he was cursed to walk the earth until the Second
Coming.

My family and I seem like typical Wandering Jews. Sure, we
don't taunt Christians and like other practicing Jews, we still await
the first coming. We don't feel cursed although we still can't forget
the impact on our lives caused by Christians who supported the
Holocaust.

To put it positively, I realize the benefits I enjoy as a "citizen
of the world" who can call any place home. Still, I often yearn for
ties to a specific spot to represent a specific home where we clearly
belong. In that frame of mind, I have envied my late friend Ivan
Glick, the scion of an Amish family in Lancaster, Pennsylvania. A
short walk from his house brought him to the homes of a dozen
relatives and the graves of his ancestors stretching back to the third
or fourth generation.

I don't think my family will ever attain such roots. Compare the
descendants of Ivan's great-great-grandfather, all living or buried
in Lancaster, with the offspring of my own great-great-grandfather
Abraham Heppner. Abraham raised eight children in the little German town of Pleschen, near Breslau. It then was part of Prussia, but
due to border corrections, it is now in Poland.

Seven of Abraham's children left Pleschen and emigrated to
America. Only Elias, my great-grandfather, remained in Europe.
Still, each generation of his line, including Elias himself, had to get
used to a different location and culture.

In 1911, when he was seventy-eight years old, Elias moved from
Pleschen to Berlin to be with his son Max, who had made the move
earlier. Even disregarding geopolitics, Pleschen and Berlin were

worlds apart sociologically. I have a letter Elias wrote to his siblings in America in which he passionately reveals the culture shock he experienced after leaving his little rural village.

After Max and Elias moved to Berlin, my family moved between countries twice more. My father, Albert, born in Berlin in 1900, fled Germany for Amsterdam, Holland, to escape the Nazis after they had come to power in Germany. I myself was born in Amsterdam in 1933.

I left Europe behind for America in 1946 to live with my aunt and uncle to attend high school in Cleveland, Ohio. I stayed in Cleveland, and I was married in 1958 to Evelyn, a Cleveland girl, although immediately after our honeymoon we moved to Columbus where we both attended Ohio State University. After graduation, we moved to jobs that took me to settle in Madison, Wisconsin (I had a fellowship there to support graduate studies), Cincinnati, Ohio, Indianapolis, Indiana, and finally found a stable career with the U.S. Government in Washington, DC, and surroundings. Its was there, in Columbia, Maryland, that our son, Albert was born in 1974.

Evelyn and I split up, and after I remarried, my second wife, Helene Hirschler talked me into moving to Switzerland in 1983 along with our young daughter, Liora, then three years old. We moved back and forth between America and Switzerland until she and her mom stayed in Switzerland permanently to let her attend a Waldorf high school. After graduation, Liora met and married a Swiss citizen, Edouard. I still travel to Europe a lot, in major part to visit Liora and Edouard and their two children, both of whom were born in Switzerland!

My citizenship was at its most tentative in my early years. Even though I was born in Amsterdam and lived there until age thirteen, I actually was a kid without a country. The Dutch authorities consistently refused to grant citizenship to me, my parents, and most other Jewish refugees from Germany. The fact that I was born on

Dutch soil made no difference to the bureaucrats. They relentlessly listed me as a German citizen because my parents had German passports.

After the Nazis installed their own crew of bureaucrats in Holland, they took away even my German citizenship. On paper, I belonged nowhere. After liberation, incredibly, the Dutch government still refused me documentation. And after I moved to America, the American bureaucrats wouldn't consider naturalizing me until I was eighteen years old.

The way my family lived ever since my great-grandfather Elias left his home in Pleschen engendered unrelieved insecurity, reflected in the fact that none of my direct ancestors acquired any owned property. Great-grandfather Elias and his son, grandfather Max, lived in rented apartments after they moved to Berlin. The next Heppner generations stayed apartment dwellers up to 1972, when Evelyn and I bought a newly built house in Columbia, Maryland.

I myself am amazing to realize, as I type this, how long I felt a strong need to stay footloose, ready to move on quickly if my Diaspora home no longer seemed safe. Rabbi Peter Tarlow, a long-term spiritual leader for the Hillel Foundation at Texas A&M, taught me that Hebrew has two (related) words for "Diaspora": *Golah* refers to geographic, physical exile; *Galut* denotes the psychological and spiritual state of exile. *Galut* means to live without norms (anomie), to feel alienation, and a sense of spiritual loneliness.

This distinction helps to understand why I was so reluctant and upset when Evelyn and I stepped into a realtor's office in Columbia, Maryland, to buy my first house. The very idea of buying a house and growing roots in the *golah* scared me so much that, from a feeling of *galut,* I lost ten pounds of body weight in the process.

Our religious congregation in Columbia dedicated our new home with the relevant Jewish ceremony, *Chanukat HaBayit*. To me, the ceremony tasted like Chinese soup, sweet and sour. It was sweet because I feel we Jews are lucky to find safe homes among the Christians in America. It was sour because I remember how rarely in our Diaspora we have been able to find and keep our Diaspora homes.

Over time, I've become less uptight and successively bought three condos without losing any weight or sleep over it. This makes me think I'm readier now to engage my Vision of Love.

5.
Jesus Talk and Proselytizing

We Jews have been proselytized so often—frequently with threats of force if we refused—that the mere mention of Jesus can make us cringe.

My friend Joy tells me that, in the company of Jews, she can stay neutral about Jesus, meaning that she can leave mention of the theological Jesus out of conversations. Not all Christians can do it like Joy. We Jews need to realize that when talk turns to Jesus, it doesn't necessarily mean that an "invitation to come to Jesus" comes next.

Conversations That Have Jesus in Them

When Jesus does comes up in a conversation, I listen carefully to grasp whether the feelings being expressed have proselytizing overtones. If so, I try to shut my ears. It isn't always easy to shake off a proselytizer, in much the same way that women can't always easily shake off a man who talks about "love" with a leer in his eye suggesting that he is bent on seducing her.

Women have to be alert to predatory males, and they learn to differentiate being hit on from a friendly talk about man-woman relationships, even if the man dares to utter the three-letter word "sex." Similarly, a Jew conversing with a Christian must differentiate between a proselytizing conversation and friendly chat about religion—even if the Christian dares to utter the five-letter word "Jesus."

Jesus talk can be enlightening. In getting to know Joy, it was essential that I let her speak freely of her relationship with Jesus. Since Jesus is important to Joy, then my understanding of what makes Joy tick has to include talk of Jesus.

Jesus Talk in the Public Arena

A different, related challenge comes up when Jesus talk crops up in the public arena, as on the day when my son was being honored in a military ceremony. The ceremony took place in rural Virginia. My late wife, Shana, son, Albert, and I were probably the only Jews in the crowd.

The commanding officer opening the ceremony said that no chaplain was on hand and that therefore he himself would offer an invocation. As usual, my body stiffened a bit just before he came to the end, hoping he would not use the ending that so excludes us. He did. Out came the words, "And this we pray in the name of our Lord Jesus Christ. Amen."

In response, I wrote a letter to the Defense Department. I indicated that I respected the sincerity of the officer leading the invocation. That said, I suggested that all officers need to be trained to speak in public with more sensitivity. Jesus Christ is not the Lord of us Jews. Praying that way violates the U.S. Constitution. The First Amendment institutes freedom of religion in the United States, and therefore an officer of the government may not favor any particular religion.

I received back a courteous response, agreeing with my position and accepting my suggestion. It was a private matter, and I carry no grudge against the officer giving the invocation; I just want his eyes opened to the fact that Jews, including my son, the honoree, are part of his America, but not part of his religion.

The issue also came up in situation that was clearly embarrassing for all concerned. It came up at the end of a panel discussion about diversity at which a Lutheran minister took part to broaden the understanding of the mostly Jewish attendees. To end the session, the moderator, my teacher Rabbi David Zaslow, gave all of us a blessing.

He then asked his colleague, the minister, whether he would add his own blessing. Looking uncomfortable, he said he would, but only if he could do it in the name of Jesus Christ.

The Jewish majority objected. The minister apparently understood our reason, but he could not overcome his need to pray in the name of Jesus. We had to do without his blessing.

I used to be annoyed and defensive in situations like that. Today, I'm happy to let people address God any way they want, and all I ask is to have that same privilege for myself. Actually, I don't ask; I just assume that right.

I'm also happy that other Jews in America have become less sensitive to Jesus and related Christian religious symbols. It's evident, for example, in an op-ed piece titled "Mysterious Times," by Stuart Schoffman, an associate editor of the *Jerusalem Report,* published in the May 9, 2003, issue of the *Jewish Times of Baltimore.*

During a visit to the United States, Schoffman celebrated Passover with his family in a private room at a big hotel. In the next room, another group was gathered for a communal Seder. It turned out this other group were messianic Jews—Jews for Jesus.

Their Seder, Schoffman found out, reinterpreted the three ceremonial matzot on the Seder table. Early in the standard Seder, it calls for breaking the middle matzo in half. One piece is hidden until it is brought out for later use during dessert. For the messianics, Jesus was the middle matzo, and its being broken was reinterpreted to symbolize Christ being broken on the cross and resurrected as Savior.

As I was reading this article, I thought that at this point, the writer would go ballistic about this Christological shift. Instead, he informed himself more about this group's practice on its website. There, he found the messianic Haggadah, published by the Lederer Foundation of Baltimore. In it, he read, "In recent years, more and more Jewish people are believing that the Messiah has come. At the same time, more and more Christians are exploring the Jewish roots of their faith." He seemed to appreciate that sentiment.

6.

Converting Between Faiths

I am still unsure exactly how to answer when a Christian asks, "Why don't you Jews want to come to Jesus?" In one of our many talks, Joy did inquire what keeps a Jew like me Jewish.

"Why do you resist salvation? she asked. "For nearly 2,000 years, you Jews have been resolute—if not to say stubborn—about sticking to your *good old religion.* Really, why is that? Just look at the recorded miracles He performed! Throughout history, there have been more books written about this one man, Jesus Christ, than any other man who has ever lived. Why would this be if He were not who He said He was: the Son of God?"

I chose the words for my reply with care, because I didn't want her to feel rebuffed and discounted. And I also didn't want to appear unappreciative when she lovingly and caring asked why I didn't want to come to Jesus.

A caring call "to come to Jesus" did convince many believers during the 2,000 years that Joy cited. In turn, those converts, made and convinced more converts by this kind of logic. So why indeed do many Jews hold out until today?

Maybe, my answer goes, they turn a deaf ear to pleas from a Christian because the offer to come to Jesus seems to derive from a need to stamp out unbelief. To them, we Jews seem to be walking billboards proclaiming doubts that Jesus is indeed the Savior. They sound like a bully dumping on a victim, not like a kind heart who wants to share a treasure with a friend.

Some true believers, of course, do indeed offer Jews what they believe and treasure, speaking out of a sense of love and without a hidden agenda. I felt Joy's deep caring when she approached me with her invitation early in our friendship. Nonetheless, she seemed to want complete acceptance of Christ as a historical personage and as a member of the Trinity—the mediator between people and God. That's the point I couldn't adopt for myself.

So we let the issue of the Holy Trinity go, and next got into a discussion of the Immaculate Conception, which I thought would be easier for us to handle. I was wrong. The minute we took it up, I ran straight into trouble.

"I believe in the Virgin Birth of Christ as a scientific fact," she declared staunchly.

"Well," I replied, "you're right on my turf with that statement. I once wrote an article about scientists who had produced an asexual turkey in the lab. They got the female to hatch an egg with a full complement of chromosomes in the nucleus instead of the usual half-portion. In nature, that happens very rarely, and even then it can't explain a virgin birth in humans scientifically."

"Oh," she said in a huff. "Does that mean you consider the Virgin Birth a fluke of nature?" Clearly, she felt attacked. "Look," she said, "I don't question your sacred beliefs. Back off from mine."

It was one o'clock in the morning, and we were waiting in line at an airport—not a good time and place to try to sort out science and religion. Insensitively, I charged ahead, getting myself in deeper.

I explained why science could never support an analogy between the Immaculate Conception and asexual turkeys. The research showed, first of all, that asexual turkey chicks don't do very well. The few chicks that hatched were all weak, often deformed. A human asexual baby on the turkey chick model would hardly qualify for *Jesus Christ, Superstar.*

I should really have noticed by then that Joy was turning me off. Instead of watching her body language, I warmed further into my topic.

"Secondly," I continued, "science has long established a reverse genetic makeup in birds. Even a perfectly formed asexual human baby would be female, not male, like a turkey chick. Since Jesus was male, he couldn't be the product of a human egg nucleus that hadn't split."

"Will you stop already?" Joy finally interrupted vocally. "Christians believe the Immaculate Conception to be a wonderful and miraculous Act of God. I don't expect you to believe that aspect of my faith, but I don't want to hear you question it. It is perfectly fine for us not to believe everything alike."

"Okay," I said. "I don't want to pour cold water on the Immaculate Conception. The Bible doesn't lecture on reproductive principles. It pleads for taking its words as an instructional or inspirational model."

"You're still being pedantic, Max," she said, "but you're getting closer to what I believe. Which is that the Holy Spirit of God was the Father of Jesus, *his only begotten Son,* as it says in Scripture. That isn't so much a scientific presentation as a spiritual truth."

Joy was right. Instead of looking to science to critique the Immaculate Conception, I can treat New Testament passages of Scripture with the same respect as Old Testament stories. Jewish interpreters do so, for example, in commenting on God's parting the waters at the Sea of Reeds when the Jewish people were running from the Egyptians. They say a guy named Nachshon bravely took the first step into the roiling waters of the Sea of Reeds before they parted, and his bravery activated the miracle.

That interpretation clearly highlights the benefits of unwavering faith and helps one experience the Vision of Love that I was urged to spread.

Why Some Christians Yearn for Abraham

As Jewish and Christian communities open to one another, more and more Christians are starting to explore conversion to Judaism. These Christian seekers generally receive an icy reception from the Jewish community, much different from the warm welcome that would-be Jewish converts receive from the Christian community.

The Jewish reserve and suspicion is deplorable, but understandable. We Jews have felt so victimized by Christians aiming to convert us that we're careful not to proselytize in reverse. A rabbi approached by a would-be convert traditionally turns away the seeker three times. Only if the seeker persists further do rabbis consider extending a supportive hand.

Some born-Christians do indeed push forward. In many cases, these Christians are in love with a Jew and want to fill in the religious gap occasioned by this love. These "in love" petitioners present a special challenge. Even rabbis who basically are open to petitioners don't want to perform a "conversion of convenience."

Refusing such a "conversion of convenience" also isn't comfortable for the rabbi because without his intervention, both members of the couple might feel forced away from Judaism. This dilemma often is resolved by requiring both the Jewish and the non-Jewish partner to go together through the instructional process for conversion. If that seems to unite them, the rabbi will go ahead with the conversion.

Other Christian petitioners approach conversion without external motivation. Typically, they have studied some aspects of Jewish practice on their own and have sat spellbound in the back rows of synagogues. When these petitioners finally approach a rabbi, they can mount convincing rebuttals to the rabbi's traditional doubts. After conversion, they typically become valuable contributors to Judaism. They are more likely than a Jew-by-birth to pursue deep study of Jewish practice and lore, and they become actively involved members of Jewish congregations.

Most rabbis encounter relatively few requests for conversion. Not so, in the case of one of my favorite rabbis, the late Rabbi Samuel Lerer, who helped thousands of people cross from Christianity into Judaism.

He operated in a special arena: The reconversion of nominal Christians whose ancestors were forced into Catholicism during the time of the Inquisition. Once called *Marranos,* which translates into English as "Pigs," they are now known by the more politically correct terms *Anousim* or *conversos. (Anousim* is Hebrew for "forced ones," and *conversos* is Spanish for "converted ones.")

To help these seekers, Rabbi Lerer had to be inventive because returning *Anousim* typically face numerous obstacles. They often live far from the nearest existing Jewish community, and even when they find their way there, mainstream Jews respond with fear. They don't want to be accused by powerful Catholic authorities of "soul hunting," particularly in Mexico where Rabbi Lerer worked.

When Rabbi Lerer occasionally was approached by Catholic petitioners who had no Jewish heritage, he expressed the standard hesitation in a uniquely loving response.

He'd say, "When you last came to Communion, did you feel a special surge of excitement as you took the wafer and let it dissolve in your mouth? Did you feel that spiritual connection?"

Often, the answer was, "Yes."

Then the rabbi would continue, "Even so, do you feel a strong pull by something you've noticed in Judaism?"

Again the answer would be, "Yes."

Then Rabbi Lerer would advise, "Please stay with what you know and what you love rather than start into something that will take you away from your family and your culture. I encourage you to explore the Jewish roots of Christianity and take that into your soul to become a better Christian." Then Rabbi Lerer would smile, look the petitioner in the eye, and conclude, "Most importantly, I want you to use your exploration of Judaism to become a good Christian—one who truly loves Jews."

The rabbi of my congregation in Florida, Marc Labowitz, also has a loving attitude toward people inquiring about Judaism. He invites them to his classes and his services and lets nature take its course, whether it leads to conversion or not. His congregation is loving and supports his approach.

Elsewhere in America, I'm sorry to say, there still is a lingering suspicion of converts on the part of Jews-by-birth. Traditional congregations often resent newcomers as "diluters of Jewish blood." Newcomers can overcome this resistance by maintaining their steadfast conviction that led to conversion. Over time, the faces of newcomers become familiar, and they integrate into the congregation.

Converts from Christianity also face resentment from their Christian friends and family. A pen pal of mine, Peggy J. Knox, expressed this challenge in searing words. (I found them on the Aleph [Jewish Renewal] website on July 10, 2008.

She wrote:

I can't count the number of times I'm asked why I did convert. I can't count the number of times I've had Christians try to bring me back into the fold, how many times I have been told I just wasn't taught right, and . . . I cannot count the number of times I've been told I wasn't a Jew, because I wasn't born a Jew.

I was raised in church. I don't mean I just went to church and Sunday school on Sunday. Christianity and the Christian way were not left at the church door or forgotten when the last Amen was sung. My ancestor is John Knox. My grandparents had twelve kids and no money, but the Bible and what was taught in it was central in their home, as well as the one I grew up in . . .

I struggled to try to believe what I was supposed to. The night I finally went to a synagogue service, I knew I had come home, and what deep trouble I was in, because I would no longer try to be what I was not. . . . I had to make decisions about what I believed and I didn't believe. I asked a lot of unanswerable questions, and . . . [still,] one of the happiest days of my life was when I became a Jew, and one of the saddest day for my family. I was disowned until my dad learned he was dying and sent for me. . . .

It's hard for most people to comprehend that belief is not constant—it fluctuates. For me, it is a daily choice to listen to *Hashem* or not; to talk with Him or let Him be. There are so many times I wish I could walk away from *Hashem,* but that's like me trying to go without oxygen—ain't gonna happen!

Belief cannot be inherited, nor given to anyone. It is as personal an issue as one can ever get. One cannot argue belief . . . and those who try to put me on the spot cannot do it. If someone asks me honestly wanting to know why I chose to be a Jew, I tell them. . . . I am not uncomfortable with anyone who has chosen to leave Judaism and become Christian, and although I don't get the other religions, it is not up to me to make a value judgment—it is their personal choice.

A friend in my other congregation, the East Bank Chavurah of Baltimore, points out that people who convert also face purely internal questions and challenges. In the book *Finding a Home for the Soul* by Catherine Hall Myrowitz, published by Jason Aronson, Inc., 1995, Cathy speaks of her "obsession with finding out who God was—if of course God existed—and the evidence seemed scanty where I was living." She found a good metaphor for her difficult inner work. She writes,

One of my quests, which seems superficial but symbolized what was going on internally, was my need to find just the right cross to wear. Would it be a crude, wooden one purchased at the '*feira,*' the [Brazilian] street market? Or a jeweled one from the Dutch miner turned precious-stone dealer? Or perhaps a simple gold cross on the thinnest of chains, unobtrusive but evident? I simply could not put Jesus and God together . . . [and I never] came to any conclusions. I never did buy a cross.

In Jewish naming ceremonies, we Jews-by-birth get special Hebrew names that stay with us throughout life. We use them, for example, when we are called upon to read or bless a Torah passage during services.

"Jewish names" consist of a person's given name, plus the name of his father and mother. Since converts don't have Jewish fathers and mothers, they use the names of Abraham and Sarah, the Jewish ancestors of all of us. Peggy Knox took the name Batsheva bat Abraham v'Sarah. Cathy Myrowitz took the name Chaya-Ruth bat Avraham v'Sarah, different from the name of her born-Jewish husband, Elliott Myrowitz, who retained the names of his blood parent, Eliyahu ben Shlomo ha-Cohen.

The new names of converts honor the common roots that unite our two faith communities. Conversion thus becomes less a rejection of Christianity and more an adoption of a common religious bond that supports my Vision of Love.

Christianity Isn't Just Judaism with a Jesus Veneer

Early Christian leaders deliberately distanced themselves from their Jewish origins. They even changed the wording they used in their religious messages.

My teacher Rabbi David Zaslow identified more than two dozen deliberate changes in terminology, starting with converting "Nazarenes," the early name for the followers of Jesus, into the term "Christians," which is so familiar to us. For the Hebrew *"Moshiach"* (Anointed), they substituted the Greek "Christos." For *Gan Eden,* the Hebrew expression that became the Garden of Eden, the redactors adopted the Graeco-Roman "Paradise." (In Greek, *parade-isos* means "enclosed place" or "park.") They even invented a new name for Jesus's country of birth. They made it Palestine, because Judea sounded far too Jewish.

Early Church leaders also developed a different mindset. Juda-ism's mindset developed in West Asia and therefore has a lot in common with East Asian religions—Hinduism, Buddhism, and the like. Christianity early on favored the mindset of the Greeks and Romans, to whom Christianity's founders wanted to appeal.

This change in outlook had a far greater impact than changed terminology. Philosophers call the Graeco-Roman worldview "dia-lectical"; they call the Eastern approach "dialogical." I call the two approaches "literal" versus "poetic," which is easier to understand.

You can see the difference in outlook even in the Christian ten-dency to conceptualize God as a personage, which we Jews have veered away from, and they call the God of the Jews "Jehovah" in the effort to make the four letters of God's name in Hebrew, YHVH, pronounceable, which traditional Jews have intentionally shied away from.

Rabbi Lerner expounded on this topic on his website, www.tikkun.org. There he said:

> The Hebrew word YHVH is a concept, not a proper name. The root of the concept is HVH, which in Hebrew [approxi-mates] . . . the present tense of the verb to be.
>
> When you put a 'yud' (Y) in front of a root of a verb in Hebrew, you are indicating future tense. So the word can't exactly be translated, but it would mean something like [mov-ing] . . . from what is to what should be . . . in accord with our God's nature to be loving, peaceful and just.

I found the same meaning in Rabbi David Cooper's writings, expressed succinctly just in the title of one of his books, *God Is a Verb* (Riverhead Books by Putnam, 1997).

We Jews have some fifty names for God that we use quite a bit; we have another fifty or so that come up now and then. For Christians, God is God and that's it.

The Jewish "God of Many Names" can be visualized as untouchable and stern when called upon with a remote name like Judge; he can come out feeling close and near and dear with a name like Beloved. Paradoxes and internal contradictions don't bother Jews a lot.

This typically Jewish worldview is reflected in the way Jews deal with the concept of "good" versus "bad." A God with fifty names can embrace both the good and the bad in human society. A God with just one name tends to deny any role in evil.

Altogether, Christianity, taking its cue from Ancient Greek philosophers, deals in absolutes. For Christians, black can never be white and gray doesn't exist. Judaism operates mostly in the gray zone. Jewish literature and Bible study involve a lot of heated discussions. Observant Jews debate "truths" that seem absolute and incontrovertible to Christians.

The divisions between Christian and Jewish faith communities are exacerbated by unintended ones. A main unintended difference derives from the fact that the Hebrew writers of Torah were poets, while Graeco-Roman interpreters among the early Christians were logicians. Poets hint at many possible truths, whereas logicians strive for precision. For example, look at the way these two protagonists take the word "spirit," which comes up very early in the Creation Story.

The English Standard Version of the Bible translates the relevant phrase, "And the Spirit of God was hovering over the face of the waters." What is nailed down as "spirit" in the English comes from *ruach* (pronounced "roo-ach") in Hebrew. However, the Hebrew has at least three other possible translations, "breath," "soul," and "wind." None of these meanings is more (or less) correct in this context. I'm boldly stating that all four concepts are contained in one Hebrew word, and you have to be a poet to wrap your mind around that.

This smorgasbord of meanings comes on top of the many out and out Biblical mistranslations that have led to misunderstandings. Christians who did the early translations often were poorly schooled by today's linguistic standards. Many never even saw the original Hebrew, but worked from a Bible that first had been translated into Greek.

Their errors were worsened by a tendency to infuse their translations with their own preconceived notions. A wry example of this is their depiction of Moses as having horns upon descending from Mount Sinai with the Tablets of the Law. The Hebrew word in the biblical description of Moses' appearance is *keren,* which has two alternative meanings—"horn" is possible, but "ray of light" is correct in this context.

The wrong choice was depicted most famously in Michelangelo Buonarroti's sculpture of Moses that still stands in the Church of San Pietro in Vincoli in Rome, Italy, today. That image, though now widely known to be an error, has persisted until today in cartoons drawn by Jew-haters.

In the first century after the birth of Jesus, leading masters on the Jewish side of the widening gap also made efforts to clarify and define the issues that separate them from the evolving Proto-Christian community.

To illustrate this by example, let's have a look at the position Jewish leaders took on undertaking abstinence and abjuring physical comforts in order to promote spiritual growth. The issue itself was not new. Keeping the soul "pure" has been an established concern since long before the advent of Jesus.

However, Torah Scripture doesn't take a firm stance on denying bodily comforts as a spiritual practice. However, early Proto-Christians adopted a stance clearly affirming that spirituality can be enhanced by the very act of bodily mortification or even self-mutilation.

Since then, Christianity has increasingly taken on the view that people who take monastic vows live the ideal spiritual life on earth. It became a holy and significant ideal to limit social contacts, avoid sex, minimize food intake, sleep in simple beds, and house one's self in modest quarters.

Self-denial led Christians to establish countless monasteries and nunneries. Monastic orders proliferated so greatly that they occupied a major stratum of society, especially after the collapse of the Roman Empire.

Meanwhile, the mainstream Jewish community increasingly distanced itself from intentional physical denial and abstinence. On the one hand, Jewish masters lavished praise on the benefits that undertaking vows of abstinence can theoretically provide, but at the same time they set up rules and regulations that made it increasingly hard for a penitent to actually take on and carry out vows of penitence. The rules started increasingly to look like provisions of a legal contract—a contract offering abstinence in return for special favors that God would confer.

The person taking on vows of abstinence came to be called a *Nazirite,* and *Nazirites* were severely warned against taking on this contractual course of action without serious forethought and rabbinic counseling. People not formally becoming a *Nazirite* were warned of the dire consequences of doing so haphazardly. See for example the succinct judgment expressed in Proverbs 18:1: "A man who isolates himself [from normative communal activities is a person who] seeks his own desire; he rages against all wise judgment."

Nazirites abide by obligations called *Nedarim* in Hebrew, obligations that go far beyond the American-English concept of "vows." *Nazirites* vow specifically to abstain from alcohol, to let head hair grow without ever cutting it, and to avoid defilement by contact with corpses. These clauses were encoded in Torah [Num. 6] and then were so expanded that the details fill an entire Talmudic tractate (subsection), which is appropriately titled *Nedarim*. A *Nazirite* who fails to fulfill his obligation can be taken into a religious court, and if convicted, he can be penalized, even though *Nedarim* are personalized, unique, and self-imposed.

The seriousness accounted to *Nedarim* comes to light whenever religious Jews make promises. To assure that their promises will not be interpreted as constituting *Nedarim,* they automatically add the phrase *"b'li neder"* (without involving any"vow") to the conversation. It makes no difference that the promise involves every-day activities. I hear Jewish men saying things like: "Honey, don't worry about picking up the kids today after school. I'll be in the neighborhood and I'll pick them up— *"b'li neder."*

To approach the issue from the positive side, just look how sumptuously middle-class religious Jewish families dine after completing morning prayers, especially on Shabbat. Traditional morning prayers themselves give thanks in general "for providing all of my needs," and continue with specific thank-you's for good clothing, calm seas by the beach, easy strides on a morning walk, and a good work-out "to keep my back nice and straight."

Despite all the talk about avoiding *Nedarim,* Jewish observance has retained practices that on the surface look like abstinence, as for example the 27-hour fast observed on Yom Kippur, the Day of Atonement. Closer examination, however, reveals that the fast is undertaken not to mortify the body but to temporarily free ourselves from tending to bodily needs, so that we can totally focus on self-examination and transformation.

I'm continually amazed at finding yet another passage in the Bible that features or refers to *Nazirites* and *Nedarim.* I also keep finding these references in secular settings, like the opera of "Samson and Delilah."

Audiences titter at the sex in the story, but I look at it more as a morality tale, intended to feature the consequences when a *Neder* vow is broken. In Scripture, [Judges, Chapters 13–16], Samson the Strongman's most dire misstep is breaking his promise to leave his hair uncut. It is presented as an important clause in Samson's contract with God because in return, God contracts to grant him enormous physical strength.

Samson's breach of promise is engineered by Delilah, who takes advantage of Samson's lust for sex and drink. Delilah is a secret agent employed by the Philistines, who at the time are in a mortal war with the Jews.

With the purpose of taking Samson out as a leader in battle, Delilah seduces him into a drunken sex orgy that leaves him in a stupor. So then Delilah calls in the barbers, and she insists that no trace of stubble be left on Samson's head so as to be sure that Samson's tremendous power is quashed. For further assurance, Philistine agents take the still unconscious Samson to Gaza and chain him to a pillar in the series of columns that hold up the roof of their huge temple.

When Samson wakes up to the horror of a shaven scalp, he calls on the remainder of his prodigious strength and yanks his chain so hard that the pillar on the other end snaps, and the whole roof crashes down. The debris that lands on Samson's head crushes his bare skull and he dies.

This dramatic, dire ending of the morality tale of Samson and Delilah seems to say, "Such is the deserved punishment for an insincere *Nazirite* who breaks his *Nedarim!*!!!"

I'll stop now with this long story about issues that show how Jewish and Christian religious beliefs and practices differ. You read enough details about the cause and effect of these differences that they will come to look less like ominous barriers. Seen as interesting topics for interfaith discussions, these differences will no longer cast a shadow on my "Vision of Love."

7.
Assessing the Divide

Christians call their Scripture a "New Testament," which suggests contention and dissension. The very derivation of the term "testament" suggests a "testy" relationship! "Testament" comes from the Latin *testis,* meaning "witness," which is the base of other English words like "attest," "protest," and "contest."

Much of the New Testament attests to preexisting lore that we Jews call *Tanakh,* an acronym of the three major biblical headings: *Torah* (law), *Nevi'im* (Prophets), and *Khetovim* (Additional Writings).

Despite numerous references in the New Testament to the *Tanakh,* in practice, early Church leaders found a lot in Torah and the rest of the Jewish Bible to protest and contest. They wanted to distance the Church from Jewish practice and they severely limited the laws of Torah. Soon they stopped talking about Torah and *Tanakh* altogether. They relegated it to an "Old Testament."

Considering the "Old" in the Old Testament

Americans don't like old stuff. We run a "throw-away" society. Every few months, we're enticed to use a "newer than new" dish soap or a hyper-updated computer program. An "Old Testament" smells of fish beyond its expiration date.

When Christians see both "testaments" bound between the same covers, they can't fail to notice that the "old" supports the "new."

The very arrangement of the text suggests that Christian beliefs are based on Jewish ones. Even if that registers, what Christians read in their combined Bible does not inform them about the Jewish belief system of today. Their Jewish reality is one that existed more than two thousand years ago.

My employer during one summer vacation from college was a devout Christian, and it didn't take long until we talked religion.

When he found out that I was Jewish, he was astounded. Not in a prejudicial sort of way—rather in an "I can't believe what I'm hearing!" sort of way. All the Jews in his experience were the Old-Testament variety, the likes of Abraham, Isaac, Jacob, and Moses. He hadn't really brought to consciousness that this old, familiar line of patriarchs had continued into modernity. If I had announced that I was an alien from Mars, I couldn't have produced a more surprised reaction.

It was a happy surprise, and our discussion stayed positive. However, it made me realize that many Christians don't seem to see the two testaments as being integrated. Instead, they view the New Testament as being built on the Old, like a cathedral in Rome built on the ruins of a temple in Jerusalem.

To tackle the true significance of "testaments" in religion, let us broaden the meaning of this term from a Jewish perspective. We Jews don't call our source of inspiration a "testament," but we do use a somewhat similar term, *B'rith* or "covenant," and our review of religious history records a whole succession of Covenants. Each Covenant in this series is a "level of belief" that builds upon its predecessors, rather than replacing them.

The first Covenant between God and humanity was the Covenant of Eden. The requirement of the covenant was twofold: "Take care of the Garden," and "Be fruitful and multiply." Not too much later in Genesis, there appears a second covenant, the Covenant of Noah, which expanded the number of requirements to seven. Third came the Covenant of Abraham. Its many strands are hard to count, but basically it affirmed the loving relationship between deity and humankind.

Then we progressed to the fourth covenant, the Covenant of Moses, which Jews believe to contain 613 commandments, including the Famous Ten.

Christians are aware of yet a fifth covenant, the Covenant of Jesus, which is what they call the "New" Testament. Like the previous covenants, the Covenant of Jesus is no repudiation of what went before.

Taken together, the series of Covenants supports the shared morality that keeps our civilization civil. Our Covenants provide a common means for religious communities to live in harmony without arguing about beliefs we don't hold in common. We need to keep our eyes focused on principles of our belief system that coincide, not on details that differ.

That's the teaching of ethicists like Charles Marsh, who point to sources in both testaments to buttress their position. The Reverend Marsh, an Evangelical minister, professor of religion, and director of the Project on Lived Theology at the University of Virginia, makes this point, for example, in an article, "God and Country," published in *The Boston Globe* of Sunday July 8, 2007. He writes:

> I fear that the gospel has been humiliated in our time. But if this has happened, it is not because the message—the good news that God loves us unconditionally in Jesus Christ, that we are freed and forgiven in God's amazing grace—has changed."
>
> To a nation filled with intense religious fervor, the Hebrew prophet Amos said, "You are not the holy people you imagine yourselves to be. Though the land is filled with festivals and assemblies, with songs and melodies, and with so much pious talk, these are not sounds and sights that are pleasing to the Lord. Take away from me the noise of your congregations, you who have turned justice into poison."

Psalm 46 tells us, "Be still and know that I am God." Dietrich Bonhoeffer, in his classic work on Christian community, *Life Together,* spoke of a silence "before the Word." He affirmed the wisdom of the Psalmist, and spoke of a listening silence that brings "clarification, purification, and concentration upon the essential thing."

After all the talk and the noise, it is time for Christians in the United States to enter a season of quietness, being still, and learning to wait on God, perhaps for the first time.

Unfortunately, the major streams of Christian theology have overlooked the succession of covenants of which I spoke. For example, look at Romans 11:16–20 NIV, where the Apostle Paul seems to waffle a bit in discussing the relationship between testaments:

> If some of the branches have been broken off,
> and you, though a wild olive shoot, have been
> grafted in among the others and now share in the
> nourishing sap from the olive root, do not consider
> yourself to be superior to those other branches.
> If you do, consider this: You do not support the
> root, but the root supports you. You will say
> then, "Branches were broken off so that I could
> be grafted in." Granted. But they were broken off
> because of unbelief, and you stand by faith.
> Do not be arrogant, but tremble.

In the end, however, Paul concludes that the old branches were broken off to make room for the new graft. They "were broken off because of unbelief, and you stand by faith."

When Christians persist in seeing their Church as a viable new branch grafted on a worn-out old olive tree, they arrive at what theologians call triumphalism, or less invidiously, a replacement theory.

Whatever it is called, I chafe under every suggestion that Judaism is no more than Pontification by Patriarchs of the Past. I deny that once Jesus and Jesuits, popes and preachers have come along, it's time for those boring begats in the Bible and those tedious tractates in the Talmud to be ignored. I invite Christians to see both modern Jewish thought and Christian theology as live parts of a tree strongly rooted in and fed by all five Covenants.

It's difficult for some Christians to understand that point. Like my employer on the farm in Ashland, they are so accustomed to seeing Jews as "Old Testament" people that they don't see us as part of the religious scene of today. Christians touring Israel exemplify this shortcoming. I learned this from my late cousin Menachem Heppner, who worked as a tour guide in Jerusalem. He said that, understandably, pilgrims want to learn about the life and concerns of Jews at the time of Jesus, and that interest is commendable. We Jews also enjoy digging in the soil of Israel for memorabilia from the last Judean kingdom.

Nonetheless, both Diaspora Jews and resident Israelis live our everyday lives in the present, and many Christian tourists don't get that point. They don't understand that the "Holy Land" that they have come to see is the present-day State of Israel.

Menachem himself played a significant part in the struggle to create the modern State. He could tell spellbinding stories about his life and weave them into stories from Scripture. However, when he started telling about challenges Israelis face today, some clients turned him off. They said, roundabout, "We don't want to hear about Jewish troublemakers who are stirring up trouble in the Middle East." The Jews of the past may be interesting to them, but not the Jews of today.

What I'm leading up to is that Torah, Talmud, and all "ancient" Jewish teachings easily fit into life situations today. They are as current as today's newspaper. They even fit into your own home. I'll give you a personal example:

I have been married to my new wife, Helena, since 2014. We have a warm relationship, but I threatened it one Friday afternoon when we had planned to go to evening religious services. I was bent on getting there on time, driven by a message drilled into me by my parents. Dad loved to quote a saying that, translated from the German, says: "Punctuality is the courtesy of kings."

I started looking for Helena early enough to have supper ready on time, but she was nowhere to be seen. Finally, I found her in bed with a mask on her face, taking a nap.

Impatiently, I woke her up. She stirred slowly and leisurely headed for the kitchen. Then I saw her mess around with food supplies and pots and pans instead of cooking with dispatch.

In a righteous voice, I said, "Will you please stop fussing and get our meal on the table?"

She responded, "I want to make our Friday night something special."

"That's great," I said, but not sounding very pleased. "If you want to do that and still leave on time, you need to set an alarm and not stay in la-la land."

"I'm doing my best!" she said back. "Can you just have a little bit of patience?"

Eventually the meal was on the table, and indeed it was special. Instead of enjoying it, I gulped it down. I wanted to leave reasonably on time, but instead of heading for the door, Helena looked for something on her iPhone. Then I blew up.

"Sit on the roof with your phone," I said sarcastically. "Go ahead and ruin a peaceful Sabbath."

"I was just checking the traffic on Waze," she responded. "What's with your obsession about time? Go by yourself if all you want to do is pester me."

I was about to escalate the rancor when I realized that my "obsession," as she called it, bruises the love that exists between us.

I understood that more deeply once we arrived at the synagogue.

(Ironically, the service hadn't even started when we got there.) The Torah *parsha* (segment) for that week was *Pinchas* (Numbers 25: 1–8), and the protagonist of that segment, Pinchas, is clearly full of self-righteous obsession. Quickly, I recognized the parallel to my own obsession about time.

Incidentally, the story of Pinchas represents a good example of how ancient Jewish teachings still apply and have been modernized to keep them so. Rabbi Peter Tarlow, my teacher whom I cited earlier, explained that verity in a lesson he shared by e-mail. He wrote:

[The plot of the Pinchas story] revolves around an incident when an Israelite man, Zimri (Hebrew, meaning "singing airhead"), brings his Midianite lover, Cozbi (Hebrew, meaning "liar"), to the Tabernacle for an illegal sexual liaison. Pinchas becomes so angry at their behavior that he takes the law into his own hands and kills both of them with his spear. To make the section even more problematical, the text makes it very clear that God is pleased by this one-man vigilante action.

When one reads the text against the background of Jewish law, however, it becomes clear that mainstream Judaism has moved far from Pinchas. Over the last 3,000 years, Jewish legal opinion has come to reject pure zealous actions and instead developed perhaps the world's most sophisticated legal system.

Pinchas never became a Jewish role model. Instead our model is Jacob, who wrestled with his own ethics and with God and from that struggle developed an ethical imperative. The lesson to be learned is that we celebrate not the zealous martyr, but rather a legal system that guarantees each person due process.

Rabbi Tarlow went on to say that if you disregard what happened within Judaism since the time we wandered in the desert, your concept of Jewish law is dreadfully out of date—and that is why I quote him here. We need to do away with misconceptions if we wish to realize my Vision of Love.

The Challenge in Interpreting the Bible

One barrier to a common understanding of the Bible is a mindset common among American Christians that has little to do with theology, dogma, or faith. Key voices call for interpretations that are literal, prosaic, and materialistic. They want a crystal-clear answer to questions like, "Is global warming caused by us or by nature?" before they roll up their sleeves and actually do something about it.

Although we Jews are exposed to the same American culture, we have managed to avoid excessive literalism in interpreting the Bible. Jewish tradition considers God's word to be a gift, a guidebook for healthy living, not a precise instruction manual for living the "right" life in today's world.

Rabbi Peter Tarlow, my teacher whom I cited earlier, pointed to this view in his Torah commentary of August 22, 2008. He said:

> The Torah section of Ekev . . . reveals how Moses has matured from a halting and inexperienced leader into a Great Leader. . . . In its review of Moses' life, Parshat Ekev reminds us that a leader is a man who patiently guides a nation and teaches it. Throughout these chapters we see a Moses who no longer dictates to Israel but instead clearly explains options and the consequences of good or poor choices. (See Deuteronomy 7:12–11:25.)

By contrast, Christian theology has tended to extract a load of guilt from Scripture, whether the passage involved is an admonition or a story with a moral. A good example of this difference with Judaic practice can be found in dealing with the so-called "Ten Commandments."

I have been plowing through a book on that topic, titled *Chiseled Words, Expressive Language: A Trip through the Ten Words of the Jewish Tradition.* The authors, all Jewish, try to bridge the gap between taking the words of the Bible as engraved in stone versus taking them as emotive expressions.

They call the copy I own "Book One" (inferentially promising us more efforts along this line), and it takes them all of two hundred pages to deal with just the primary issues raised by the Big Ten. (The book is in Dutch—*Gebeitelde Woorden, Sprekende Taal: Verkenning van de Tien Woorden in de Joodse Traditie,* from Hilversum Publishers, 1996—but that doesn't matter for our purpose because Dutch is nearly as prosaic as English, and the Dutch mind is nearly as literal.)

First of all, the authors point out that the famous list of moral strictures doesn't particularly contain ten items. The Hebrew text isn't numbered, and a look at the content in the original shows you various possible divisions.

Hebrew commentators classify the content under as few as seven and as many as seventeen different headings. Ten, according to the Dutch authors, was probably selected to connect the "commandments" with similar ten-part listings in the Bible, such as the ten-part description of creation. Only much later did the number ten take meaning in terms that appeal to Western literalists. So, the list itself doesn't stand as monolithically in the original as in its Western interpretations.

Secondly, the Hebrew authors didn't see their list of strictures as commandments. The title "Ten Commandments" appears nowhere in Torah. It was added later by the editors of Christian Bibles. Actually, the Hebrew for the items in the list is *Dibrot,* which usually is translated as "things" or "words," but in this context, better as "pointers." They are pointers for living the healthy, moral life. They say that, in the writer's opinion, God supports those of us who deal respectfully, even lovingly, with their relatives, friends, and neighbors.

For example, the coveting bit at the end doesn't mean God is looking into your head to see whether you covet your neighbor's ass. Rather, the "pointer" in this case points out that you will live a happier and more fulfilling life if you keep your eyes on your own goals and opportunities, not on trying to keep up with the Joneses (or the Cohens) next door.

In sum, Jewish commentators do not see God as a vengeful executioner. God does not impose Himself to inquire into your moral status. Even His judgment at the end of your days is metaphoric; Judaism teaches that you make your own Heaven or Hell.

In providing us with pointers, regardless of whether we count them as seven, ten, or seventeen, God puts suggestions out there for pondering the moral life. If you pick up the pointers right and use them right, you have made good use of God-given tools for living the fulfilled life. If not, then you will be the poorer for it. It is important to take these pointers seriously, but not guiltily. They are not meant to make you miserable or apprehensive, but to enrich your life.

Even with a biblical passage that's a story rather than an explicit commandment, a literal interpretation can become a problem. For example, take the story of the problem King David encountered when he tried to move the old Ark of the Covenant, which had been in storage, to Jerusalem on an oxcart. The Biblical author relates how one man steadied the ark when the oxcart hit a bump. Touching the ark was apparently a taboo. As punishment, Uzzah, the poor fellow who did it, was consumed by a fireball (2 Samuel 6:1–11).

Now, even if the man in the story had been touching the ark in a disrespectful way—and the context shows otherwise—fiery death doesn't seem like a fitting punishment. With a literal reader's eye, you can easily have yourself believing that God will knock you into a fireball if you accidentally screw up a major task in a minor way.

Even with a Jewish reader's eye, I'm not sure what moral I can draw from this story. Possibly, the idea is to imbue respect for The Law (the Torah).

Whatever the true message may be, it is not intended to make your life miserable. The challenge in interpreting the story is drawing something from it to enrich your life today.

I've been saddened to hear about Christian interpretations that take the opposite tack. That is particularly true when you examine the notion of Original Sin as a spin on the experiment by Adam and Eve with the fruit of the Tree of Knowledge in the Garden of Eden.

Here's how a fire-and-brimstone interpretation, particularly common in America, was presented in an article in the *New Age Journal*. Brenda Peterson writes in the October 1993 issue about a sermon she heard from a Baptist minister in rural Montana. Vividly she describes the scene, dating to her childhood in 1958, as she and her two sisters take in the minister's message:

> We three sisters were sitting in a pew, legs dangling, our shoulders hunched over in fear, as if awaiting a blow.
>
> The preacher shouted, "It was Eve who ate that apple from the Tree of Knowledge of Good and Evil. And in going against God's will, in eating the fruit poisoned with mortality, that woman condemned us all to exile from God's Garden. She listened to the snake and her own sinful self, instead of her sweet Lord!"
>
> We shuddered, we three terrified sisters, little descendants of Eve. "Little women," the preacher went on to declaim, "[you] have to work especially hard for our Lord's redemption. [You] were the first in all creation to go against His divine will."
>
> My younger sister whispered in my ear, asking, "Do you think God will ever forgive us for eating that stupid apple?"

Peterson comments that, even today, she feels "happy hopelessness" in being an unforgiven female.

Heavens! How far removed are the three little girls in Montana from my forefathers who first told the tale in the Sinai desert. They were spinning it in the spirit of Rudyard Kipling describing *How the Elephant Got Its Trunk*. The forty-year wanderers were questioning why they were sweltering in the hot sands when, instead, they might be luxuriating in a lush Garden of Eden. They couldn't deny the sweat on their brow, so they made up a story of "how come."

Over the years, Jewish commentators have imbued their "how-come" story with deeper meaning, and I think that this is appropriate. They say this story teaches that every discovery has a cost. If we wish for knowledge of good and evil, we create a world with judgment in it. And, by extension, if we wish to ride around in horseless carriages, we create a world with exhaust gases in it.

To put things in terms of another Eastern tradition, once a genie is out of the bottle, we can't put it back. But we're not helpless or hopeless once we know good from evil. It prompts us to look for ways to soften judgment. It also prompts us to look for ways to counteract exhaust gases.

Unfortunately, the Baptist minister who preached about original sin turned the moral on its head. Instead of softening judgment, his exegesis made judgment harsher. In the process, he changed a loving, nurturing God into a mean monster. At best, he gave three innocent little girls "happy hopelessness."

We Jews don't understand "happy hopelessness." As Hershel Jonah Matt put it in a modern-day Jewish prayer, "Keep us, O Lord, from sinking into helplessness and hopelessness. Teach us, O Lord, to know that when You granted us the power to sin, You blessed us also with the power to repent. We need not continue on in all our sinful ways."

Jewish interpreters hold that the fruit that Eve shared with Adam was sweet, not sour or bitter, as in the view of the minister from Montana. The sweetness, Jewish lore says, comes to us as wisdom. Our interpretation says that God smiled when the First Couple tasted the "forbidden fruit" because God knew that, at this point, they could handle responsibility. He no longer had to mollycoddle a couple of naïfs in a Garden of Eden.

There are several Torah passages far more explicitly fear-inspiring than the Expulsion from the Garden of Eden—for example, the string of curses in Deuteronomy 27. However, the Jewish take on even these dire passages is instructive, rather than damning. Here's how my teacher Rabbi Peter Tarlow put it in an online Torah study on September 19, 2008:

> If we read the text carefully, we note that the text is not about punishments but rather is suggesting that consequences are a necessary part of a civil society. If we were to live in a world without consequences, then we would revert to a system of *Tohu va'Vohu* (the Bible's word to describe the state of 'total chaos prior to creation'"). If Genesis is about G'd's reversal of entropy, of bringing order out of chaos, then *Ki-Tavo* warns us about the negative consequences of turning order into chaos.
>
> Rather than seeing G'd as portrayed in this weekly section as angry, we might choose to see a caring G'd who gives us the right to choose and the knowledge to know what the consequences of our actions will be. Rules and consequences instead of [mere] capriciousness mean that we have the chance (but not the promise) to live meaningful lives.

Jewish tradition can comfortably fit Scripture into everyday life, even for a people who follow a strictly Orthodox lifestyle. One branch of my family fits that model. Their home has a mezuzah on every doorway and passageway. Depictions of great teachers hang on the walls, along with a photo of "the Rebbe," their personal teacher and rabbinical guide. Prayer books and religious references line every bookshelf. Prayer guides sit by every relevant appliance—the prayer for washing hands hangs by every sink and faucet. Family members rush to do the required prayer service three times a day and then to lessons and more lessons to understand Torah and God's will more perfectly.

I paint this background of their life to show that no anguish comes with it, just dedication. If they make a doctrinal mistake, they laugh it off after resolving to do better next time. They discuss aspects of their religious belief as part of their lives, much as they discuss the catch from their latest fishing trip. They struggle with doctrine like they struggle with a fish on their fishing line. They work at it, but they never, ever anguish about it. If they are worried about whether they're handling things right, they consult the rabbi.

They are more likely than me to take Bible stories literally. They may not be as quick as I to focus mainly on the grace I see in Bible stories. However, we're both together when it comes to reading inspirational stories that affirm life. Jewish Orthodox authors call, again and again, for humans to be God's partners in continuing His creation. God is depicted as a Father who delights in his human creations and wishes them happiness and success.

This type of interpretation supports my belief that even the negative-sounding Bible passages have to be seen in a positive light. They are a connection between heaven and earth and an invitation to embrace and deepen our spirituality.

Not that certain Bible passages don't cause me problems, even though their literal meaning seems clear. Look at the concern about "spilling your seed," which gets a great deal of disapproval in the Bible story about the sons of Jacob. I wrote a play on this episode once, so it's clear that I do not consider it insignificant. I do, however, dig below the surface to find significance for the passage in my life.

On its face, the passage seems to condemn masturbation. When I was younger, I did masturbate, so I had to ask myself whether that was wrong. I decided that it wasn't. Physicians and psychologists consider masturbation acceptable and even constructive for people without access to other sexual release.

Instead of drawing guilt from the passage, I look at the context under which it was written. At the time, tribes surrounding the Jewish nation venerated human ejaculate as part of a fertility rite used in the Temples of Baal. This practice filled the authors of the passage with disgust.

With that understanding, I see the condemnation as relevant, but only in the past. Neither my time nor my location puts me anywhere near idolatrous Temples of Baal. I don't have sacrilegious neighbors that tempt me in this way. The passage doesn't apply to me today. However, I won't have to go far to find a preacher who loudly condemns masturbation because the Bible seems to condemn it. I am suggesting that we give this type of condemnation less power.

The New Testament presents its own doctrinal problems, many of them requiring accepting a certain belief rather than embracing or avoiding a certain practice, such as masturbation, for instance. My heart cries about Christian hearts anguishing over concepts like whether one should take the Immaculate Conception literally, as I mentioned earlier. I hope that, by looking over the fence at Jews, doctrinally challenged Christians can salve their conscience.

We Jews have a longer tradition of Bible interpretation, and, over time, we have come to see the basic message in Scripture as a call to action, while Christians gravitate to hearing a call to belief and right thinking. Both are important, and we can learn from each other.

On our side, we Jews can learn not to be so focused on action that we overlook the spiritual side of Scripture. In our preoccupation with getting things done, we risk missing the deep spiritual nourishment that Christians find in Scriptural words. And together we can deal with issues in our lives, cited in Scripture, that are not as clear on the face of it as the one concerning, say, masturbation.

Take the issue of dealing with the occult, which my friend Joy likes to call "Divination." She once wrote me:

The occult is clearly defined in Scripture. God's chosen people (into which I am grafted through faith) were somberly instructed not to involve themselves in divination.

I boil it all down to two things:

- One, it seems that divination counterfeits everything God has given us in experiencing Him and His power. I believe there is danger in connecting with unseen forces, among which I would include astrology, fortune-telling, necromancy, and inductive divination, as by consulting crystals to ferret out the unknown. Ha! I know Christians who use bibliomancy to unlock secrets in the Book of Revelations.

- Two, conversely, we can enrich our religious experience by connecting with God Himself.

For me, that includes prophecy, laying on of hands for healings, and gathering inspiration, knowledge, and discernment through prayer and meditation. All these evidence a sole desire to gain a richer attachment to God and to do His will—primarily to "be touched by God" and to touch lives with love.

God is a "jealous God" in the finest sense of the word; he can be "provoked to jealousy" through idolatrous behavior. Such figures of speech point to the intensity of God's affection for those whom He fervently loves and designs to be His own.

Jealousy always involves a triangle. Here the triangle is God, us, and occult powers. The question begs, "Are we going to be obedient to God's will? Or are we going to seek fellowship, enjoyment and direction for our current and future life through divination, which means we are seeking out other unseen powers?"

I understand Joy's concerns, but I'm loath to throw out all aspects of "divination," the good along with the bad. For example, in engaging me on this topic, Joy took issue with the Jewish Renewal practices of celebrating the new moon.

She challenged me, "Are you stooping into adoring nature instead of praying to God?"

"Depend on how you look at it," I replied. "To us, blessing the new moon is a way to enlist nature to enhance spirituality."

"Oh, yeah," she came back challengingly. "Well, how then you explain your dancing with the Torah, kissing the Torah, and putting a finger on a Portion to divine what it portends for the finger-pointer. Do you folks actually read the Torah?"

"Yes," I answered, "we read the Torah and discuss the portions that we read. We dance with the Torah to express the joy we find in it, and we kiss it to express the love we find in it. Innovative practices should be evaluated based on the direction into which we take them."

I meant that if the Torah and the moon become God rather than representing channels to God, then we've crossed the line to idolatry, the practice Joy condemns as "counterfeiting God." All Jewish prophets and rabbinic interpreters would agree with her.

Joy's critique went on to challenge what seemed to her even more esoteric practices, like necromancy—communicating with the dead.

Joy said, "Of course you know that necromancy is expressly forbidden by Torah. How to you wiggle your way around that?"

"Don't get stuck in blanket condemnation" I pleaded. "What you call necromancy actually became a personal issue at one time in my life. Let me explain how far I went down that road and where I decided to stop."

I told joy that my trip started unintentionally. At the time, my then-wife, Evelyn, was painfully struggling with the death of her aunt Rose. One night, Evelyn awoke me to tell me full of wonder, "Max! Aunt Rose is here."

"What?" I said sleepily.

"I see her spirit," Evelyn said. "She's come back to visit me."

I groaned and muttered, "It was a dream. Just go back to sleep."

"No," Evelyn said, firmness and assurance in her voice. "Wake up, Max. You've got to see this. She is here. Her spirit is here. She is wearing her favorite outfit, her jewelry, just as I remember her."

"Oh," I said, and tried to focus. "Where should I look?"

"She's by the closet," Evelyn said. She got more excited. "Now she's talking," she reported.

"Really?" I said. "I don't hear or see a thing."

"I hear her," Evelyn said. "I hear her clearly. She's saying, 'Evelyn, dear. Don't worry about me. I'm doing fine where I am. I am in another place, but I love you just the same.'"

They conversed, apparently by thought transference, totally out of my range, and Evelyn mainly commented on Aunt Rose's movements. Finally, she disappeared through the closet.

It wasn't a one-time visit. Aunt Rose came back repeatedly, always in the early hours of morning; sometimes Evelyn woke me up to alert me to what was happening. Other times, she just reported at breakfast.

The effect of their conversations was that Evelyn calmed down. Her heart was at peace, knowing that Aunt Rose's spirit rested peacefully in a safe place.

Then, Aunt Rose's nocturnal visits took a new turn. She introduced other spirits, relatives who had died earlier.

I best remember the visit of my Uncle Roger Madol. He is a relative who died years before I met Evelyn. I can't remember that we two had ever talked about Uncle Roger before his spirit appeared, but even so, Evelyn described him exactly as I had known him: A roly-poly, soft-spoken but determined man.

Uncle Roger led a dashing, adventurous life. I loved being with him and listen to his stories, but I saw him only rarely.

I was disappointed about our lack of contact. I yearned to feel and sense him the most after he had been appointed my legal guardian after my father died. I was only 11 years old; he lived in London while I lived in Amsterdam, and I was too young to visit him by myself. My mother took me to visit him in London him only a time or two.

Without ever saying so, I felt disappointed and abandoned because Uncle Roger would have had no trouble coming to me. He was a well-known historian and reporter, and as a single man, he was free to travel anywhere. However, he never came to visit me. I felt him present in my life as an attractive but distant figure while I wanted him as a father figure,.

Uncle Roger died suddenly, when I was in college in Wisconsin, and I cried silently and alone because I couldn't get to his funeral in London. It got worse when afterwards I discovered that in his will Uncle Roger didn't leave me anything, not even a personal memento.

So when his spirit came to visit, I realized how incomplete my feelings were toward him. I was glad for the opportunity that, with Evelyn as an intermediary, I could tie up some loose ends with a man whom I dearly loved but who had seemed to forget about me when I most needed him.

Gradually, Evelyn turned into a full-blown medium. We researched mediumship together and also looked into some related aspects of the occult, until we came across automatic writing. I felt drawn to that, because I could be involved. Evelyn would contact the departed, and I would be the vehicle whose hand would write down their remarks.

We followed the directions in the guidebook we found in the library, and it didn't take long before I the pen in my hand started making autonomous movements. An unknown spirit was taking over. Neither of us had any idea who he was or why he was contacting us.

When my hand stopped moving, we decided to look at what we had produced. At first glance, it was unintelligible scribble. Then I had an inspiration. I suspected that I had written a word in mirror image and upside down. Turned around and in the mirror, the word was clear. It said, "Help!!!"

Our hair raised on end, and we realized we were in over our depth. We returned the reference book to the library and threw away our equipment.

However, that didn't change the fact that both of us had found peace from contacting the departed. We came to appreciate channels and levels of existence not ordinarily open to our senses. Accessing these channels and opening up our depth of perception is more than mere "divination" or silly necromancy.

In fact, Joy and I both are familiar with the Kabbalah, a whole field of inquiry well within Judaism that deals with the occult. I can't deny that some of Kabbalistic investigations come close to sacrilege. In desperation engendered by senseless, incessant persecution, Jewish mystics have literally attempted to force the hand of God.

Setting limits in this area is a valid topic of discussion, both for Christians and Jews. Any person of faith should be free to expand upon Scripture, but none of us should depart from it so far that we lose sight of the central core of belief that Scripture represents for us.

As Joy once wrote me, "Scripture reading is vital to my existence, and I have found continuing comfort in it. It has consistently provided me with a sense of love, peace, and 'Presence.' I ponder and value the words of sages who, centuries before me, experienced blows and hammering throughout life—and still kept believing that God was good and a blessed controller of all things."

I can only say "Amen" to that.

The Advantage of Religious Diversity

America derives strength from diversity, and we Jews contribute our share. I don't speak here mainly of Jonas Salk, Albert Einstein, and other Jewish luminaries. I very much include ordinary Jews like myself who make my neighborhood culturally richer, not because

I'm a good physician or physicist like Salk or Einstein, but because I am a good Jew.

Similarly, it isn't enough for Jews to appreciate Christians like Mother Theresa and Abraham Lincoln. Of course, we value works for the poor and sick in India and outstanding leadership at the helm of our own nation. Yes, both of these celebrated heroes were devoted Christians, but we Jews need to give credit as well to millions of unsung Christians who are open-minded and kind.

We Jews don't even realize that members of our faith community have a significant outside impact. I found a case in point in a letter to the editor of the *Jewish Times,* a weekly newspaper in Baltimore, dated August 24, 2007. Commenting on an obituary that had run the previous week, the letter began, "With the passing of Rabbi Dr. Leivy Smolar, the Baltimore Jewish community, indeed world Jewry, has lost a towering intellect . . ."

As I read this, I wondered, *Why didn't the writer say 'the world' instead of 'world Jewry'? Our entire society loses when a towering intellect passes.*

What's true for Rabbi Smolar is equally true for those of us who aren't famous. If we contribute well, we add to the common good, and everyone benefits. I don't remember ever hearing about Rabbi Smolar before seeing his death notice, but I still benefited from his influence like everyone else in our area, and indeed the world!

Open appreciation and deep understanding between Christian and Jewish communities will make everyone's life more joyful. Beams of love from the church on their way to the synagogue should cross with similar beams of love traveling in the other direction.

Christians with pride in Christianity should be happy there is such a thing as Jewish pride. And Jews with pride in Judaism should be happy there is such a thing as Christian pride. We all should keep our eyes open so we notice each other's accomplishments, and we should keep our hearts open to the happiness these accomplishments generate.

Christians and Jews have developed separate cultures, even though we have lived side by side for nearly two thousand years. We Jews have preserved from the past and nurtured into the present a unique way of life. So have Christians, of course, and Jews do well to recognize this.

However, it's crucial for caring Christians to realize that the cultural aspects of Judaism go deeper because Jews are a people as well as a religion. If all Catholics were Italians, you'd have a parallel. However, the Irish are just as Catholic, and culturally the two peoples differ materially. Add to that the difference between Protestant groups—compare a Methodist with a Baptist—and the spread of both cultural and worshipping aspects of Christianity come clearly into view.

Although Judaism also contains groups with cultural differences, what makes us unique is a deep sense of peoplehood. Ingrained in our culture and worship is an ardent, oft-repeated, and deep desire to return to "the Land," which is Israel. Without a true understanding of this sense of peoplehood, you can't capture a key aspect of Judaism.

As my late cousin, Menachem Heppner, who often lectured about Judaism in Christian venues, put it (in personal correspondence):

> You are Jewish, not because you belong to a "Jewish Religion," but because you were born Jewish, much as an Italian is born Italian and a Frenchman is born French.
>
> Christianity is based on a belief in Christ, just as Islam is based on a belief in Mohammed. These are religions from which you can change along with a change in your beliefs.
>
> Judaism you cannot change. Even if you join the Church, you still are Jewish under Jewish law. You will be a Jew who lives with Christians, just as you can be an Italian who lives with Americans, or a Frenchman who lives with the Irish. You retain your origins.

I would add that Jewish culture also includes a view on proper human relations, values, ethics—even problem-solving.

I'm not the first to raise the point that Jewish values complement Christian values and as such add to the well-being of society as a whole. Hugo Grotius, a well-known seventeenth-century thinker from Amsterdam, the city where I was born, wrote:

> It is obvious that God wishes the Jews to live somewhere, and if such is the case, then why not here? What is of great importance is that the Christian religion should receive some advantage from the Jews.
>
> Two factors must be taken into account: The good of the Christian religion and the good of the State. Anything connected with these aims should be permitted to Jews and Christians alike.

Our Jewish way of life enhances our society's adaptability, which is essential for progress and even for survival. Even a small minority can increase adaptability.

Let me explain this with an analogy from animal genetics. Open the door to a modern chicken house, and your eyes light upon a sea of uniformly white chickens that have been genetically designed to lay our standard white breakfast eggs. We've become so used to uniformity in chickens and eggs that we have almost forgotten that there used to be laying hens of various hues, as well as eggs of varying colors.

Nonetheless, some specialty farms still preserve the old genetic lines, like the old Rhode Island Red of long ago. The minority Reds are the "Jewish chickens." The majority Standard-Bred Whites are the "Christian chickens."

The analog shows that when new environmental factors or diseases arise in the poultry world, the Standard-Breds may lack specific genes needed to resist the threat. In that case, breeders have to fall back on genes from days of yore. Similarly, human society also faces challenges now and again that defy standard Christian solutions. Many of these challenges can be met by the alternative culture that the Jews have preserved over the ages.

Many Americans already recognize Jewish contributions. Interestingly, this was revealed by the same Anti-Defamation League survey I mentioned earlier. Results showed that 65 percent of the two thousand respondents agreed that Jews "contribute much to cultural life" in America.

Influential individual Christians also have published outspoken appreciation for Jewish contributions to society. Here's a quote from William Rees-Mogg, former Editor-in-Chief for *The Times of London* and a member of the House of Lords.

He said:

One of the gifts of the Jewish culture to Christianity is that it has taught Christians to think like Jews. Any modern man who has not learned to think as though he were a Jew can hardly be said to have learned to think at all.

In sum, I yearn for Christians to grasp that preserving Judaism is in their self-interest. To the extent that this is coming true already, my Vision of Love is already being realized.

The Trouble with Merging Traditions

On my spiritual journey, I discovered that merging one faith into another doesn't work.

My discovery came as a shock.

Even though my birth family is Jewish, part of my upbringing is Catholic. As I've explained, the Catholic portion comes from my foster mother, Dina Janssen, who sheltered me from the Nazis on her farm.

Emblematic of Dina's faith were figurines of the Holy Family and a sizable contingent of saints that she kept around the house. I came to love these figures and the sense of peace they emanated. Although I was too young then to fully realize this, to me the figurines came to represent the unwavering love that my foster mother beamed on me.

After World War II ended and I left the farm, I greatly missed Dina's figurines. The fear that I might lose them forever hit me hard when Dina died. Ria, my youngest foster sister, called me with the sad news, and without censoring the thought, I asked her to please save one of my foster mother's figurines for me. She promised she would.

When I visited her some time later, and she showed me the figurine, I was dumbfounded. Not because it was Mother Mary, but because it didn't look ethereal, the way I remembered it. It was much larger than I recalled, and its plaster-of-Paris body showed its age with many chips and scratches.

When my rational mind returned, I came to realize that this good-sized figurine could not reasonably fit into my home in Pikesville, a predominantly Jewish suburb of Baltimore. Its presence would require constant explanations to startled Jewish friends. Sadly, I had to leave the figurine in my erstwhile home in the Netherlands.

I consoled myself with a painting by Krissa Marie Lopez, who used Native American imagery, not the familiar European depiction, to represent the Virgin Mother. Her work, titled *Nuestra Señora de La Paz,* still hangs above my desk as I write this.

I like it, but it's not powerful enough to dispel my basic problem with mixed symbology. This problem still pursues me, raising its head even as an apparently simple dispute in my Florida condo building.

Our residents' association maintains a bulletin board for notices and messages. One Easter season, Manny, then the head of the Sunshine Committee, posted a well-meant "Happy Holiday" message that strongly offended one of our Jewish neighbors.

Manny took down the poster on orders from the condo president and brought it to me. Frustrated and confused, he asked me what about the poster could have caused such a strong negative reaction.

I kept the poster in my files because it so exemplifies misunderstandings caused by mixed symbology, so I can still describe it for you accurately. It has two illustrations clipped from religious journals, one arranged above the other. The top image shows a Seder plate with Stars of David in its borders. It was captioned: *Not only once have they risen to destroy us, but [they have tried it] in every generation. But the Holy One, blessed be He, always delivers us from their hands.*

The lower image is of a huge cross, superimposed on a rising sun. It was captioned simply: *He has risen.*

Separately, the two images seem non-threatening and uncontroversial. What I think bothered the Jewish neighbor is that the Christian symbol was pasted above the Jewish one, so that together the captions promulgated a thought sounding like: *God saved the Jews at the original Passover, but none of that matters now that Christ has risen.*

I tried to comfort my neighbor, but I couldn't really relieve his dilemma. Looking back on it, I suggest, "Let's put all that jazz aside and let's work instead to actualize my Vision of Love.

8.
Holidays and Togetherness

The Challenge of Christmas

Because mixing religious symbols doesn't work for me, it's hard for me to deal with the annual appearance of Christmas in December. I'm not out to steal Christmas—I'm no Grinch, the grouchy character that Dr. Seuss created, who tries to put an end to Christmas by stealing Christmas gifts from little kids.

I appreciate Christian friends who invite me to come see their decorated Christmas tree and the pile of colorfully wrapped presents waiting to be opened on Christmas morning. I hope to continue receiving such friendly invitations, and I feel no pressure when I'm invited.

The pressure that I truly feel comes from the clash between Christmas and Chanukah, and if you need proof that other Jews also feel that pressure, come next December to my neighborhood in Baltimore and gape at a large house that has annually gets photographed and reported on in the press. The owner of the house festoons it from roof to ground level with electric candles, and he puts even larger candles, one more for each night of Chanukah, into a huge *Menorah* (candelabra) on his front lawn.

People started to call it the "Chanukah House," because it obviously tries to match the annual blaze of lights on "Christmas Street,"

a block of townhouses in mid-town Baltimore that is dazzlingly fes-
tooned with Christmas decorations.

Of course, one decorated villa can't compete with a block of
blazing lights, especially since the "Christmas Street" light show is
enhanced by a mass of other Christmas decorations in that neighborhood. I maintain that just as the Chanukah House cannot outshine
the Christmas Street, Chanukah even at its best can't compete with
the splendor with which Christmas shines forth.

There is no need even to attempt to upgrade Chanukah. As a
Jewish holiday, it appears only as a minor blip on the Jewish religious calendar. It merits no citation in the Torah and only minor
comments in the Talmud. Ironically, it's Christians who canonized
the Chanukah story in the Christian Bible as *The Book of Maccabees.*

Chanukah is accorded little attention, even by strictly observant
Jews. They light candles, put them on a windowsill facing the street,
and for the rest pretty much ignore Chanukah. Jews who started to
raise Chanukah to the level of "a Jewish Christmas" were trying to
compensate Jewish kids for missing out on decorating Christmas
trees, ripping open Christmas gifts below the tree branches, and
enjoying a festive dinner with favorite relatives and friends.

Even if we succeed in compensating Jewish kids at Christmas
time with a heap of presents, we Jews can't escape a world that still
tries to make Chanukah the "Jewish Christmas." That realization
hit me hard each Christmas during the years when I belonged to
the Parents Club of the Waldorf School, which my daughter Liora
attended from grades K to 6. During the rest of the year, I found joy
in wandering the halls of this culturally rich school, listening to the
sounds of music that poured out from each classroom. The sounds
of Christmas music, however, grated on my ears.

The Parents Club tried to accommodate the sizable minority of
Jewish parents. They tactfully renamed the Christmas music program the "Holiday Festival," and tried to be fair in selecting a mix
of Christmas carols and Chanukah songs for the program.

I appreciated the attempt, but to me it sounded like trying to squeeze jazz numbers into a Beethoven concert. Chanukah ditties are as silly as *dreydl* games, and mixing them in with sonorous Christmas carols makes it seem as if ditties are the best music we Jews have to offer.

I spoke about my feelings at Parents Club meetings, and the non-Jewish majority listened with empathy. Eventually, late in Liora's tenure at the school, the Jewish minority was encouraged to set up a support group to deal with all challenges posed by having Jewish kids in a school with deep Christian roots.

Nonetheless, I hope that other groups continue to explore workable solutions. I like the model of *De Dag van Sinterklaas* (Santaclaus' Birthday) that the people of Holland developed and gives all Dutch kids equal access to a joyful year-end holiday.

The word Dutch word *Sinterklaas* already has crept into American parlance as Santaclaus, so maybe we can build on that. Even though the word "Saint" is hidden the holiday's name and Saint Nicholas' birthday has been recognized for ages as a Catholic Saint's Day, the Dutch holiday with his name is totally secular, totally cultural, and wildly popular. December 26 is reserved for purely religious ceremonies.

The traditional date for Santaclaus' birthday is December 6, but the fun in Holland starts on the eve before. That night, Dutch children fill their wooden shoes with hay and set it out as a treat for the white stallion on which *Sinterklaas* rides over the rooftops while dropping gifts down the chimney. That's how I got my first bicycle, although at the time I didn't understand how Santa got a gift of that size down the chimney.

I'll always be grateful to the good saint for that gift alone, and I can recover that childhood excitement about the advent of *Sinterklaas* even in the United States. The immigrant Dutch community in South Florida annually arranges a *Sinterklaas Feest* (Feast of Santa Claus) for its young folks. I went there once to recover the wonder of my childhood. I eyed the traditional delicacies (like *poffertjes,* or mini pancakes) with joyous reminiscence, even though I can't eat them anymore with an eye to my diabetes.

Celebrating Light

Many cultures have developed a holiday at year-end to brighten the darkness of midwinter and to plead with the sun not to altogether abandon us to an eternal night. John Spong and Jack Daniel Spiro, an Episcopal priest and a Reform rabbi, respectively, took up that theme in a modest volume called *Dialogue: In Search of Jewish-Christian Understanding.* They explain (pages 105 and 106):

> Both Chanukah and Christmas . . . use light as a major symbol. Both speak to the ancient hopes of human beings that truth will banish falsehood and that light will banish darkness.
>
> Among our primitive human ancestors, the approach of the winter solstice gripped their lives with shivery fear. . . . They could only watch with anxiety as they . . . literally wondered if light itself were passing out of existence.
>
> Then there came that day [of relief] . . . barely noted in our scientific world as the shortest day in the year, December 21. But for our ancient forefathers, that day was an occasion of . . . wild celebration, and of divine worship . . .
>
> And so it is that in most major religions there is a holy day or a holy season that marks the coming of light into the darkness of winter. . . . It is not surprising that Chanukah is called the "festival of lights," nor is it surprising that the Christmas story is told with stars shining in a black sky with . . . heavenly light splitting the darkness of night. . . . Taking that experience of light [driving away darkness], we [can] give it content; and it becomes our revelation, our tradition, our truth.

Chanukah is that for the Jews; Christmas is that for Christians . . . . The tradition is different. But we can see in both Christianity and Judaism a common yearning, a common humanity, and a common hope. We believe that behind the diverse traditions of men there is a common God who calls us all to come to him by whatever path we walk.

I could go for a program based on that convergence, and songs already have been composed on that theme. The Waldorf School Festival of Lights actually included one of my favorites, originally composed in Hebrew. The English lyrics are as follows:

Celebrating Light

We have come to banish night
Banish it with candlelight.
Each of us is one small light,
But together we shine bright.
Go away darkness, vanish night,
We applaud the feast of light.

Light also can represent spirituality. I experienced this in a dream, where I searched for *Tsitum,* an aspiration I didn't know in waking life.

I meet a kabbalist in Israel, who offers to take my wife and me to the city of Beer Sheva, to show us the Tsitum. *As we approach the* Tsitum, *we see a mix of fire and light issuing from a fantastic container. The scene takes my breath away. The* Tsitum *is all orange and yellow beams of light with sparks flashing into, across, and along with one another from all directions. I want to call it fireworks, but that's not magnificent enough. I'm overwhelmed by the luminosity.*

Tsitum sounds very Hebrew, but asleep or awake, I didn't know a translation for it. Even my Hebrew-speaking friends didn't know.

It isn't in the Hebrew lexicon. From the context of the dream, I concluded that *Tsitum* means Sacred Light.

One of my teachers, Dr. P. M. H. Atwater once spoke of a light like that as, "A million suns of compressed love dissolving everything unto itself, annihilating thought and cell, vaporizing humanness and history into the one great brilliance of all that is and all that ever was and all that ever will be. . . . You can no longer believe in God, for belief implies doubt. There is no more doubt. None."

That concept of light at year-end excellently blots out concerns like my discomfort with Christmas and illuminates my Vision of Love.

Finding Common Ground at Easter

I kept on with my search for a holiday that could seamlessly unite Christians and Jews; and placing Passover with Easter came to mind. They seemed an auspicious couple with a lot in common:

• They uniquely converge on the calendar.

• They share an underlying theme: the bounty of nature and the fecundity of spring, featuring spring blossoms, delicious eggs, and frisky lambs.

• Passover as a Jewish observance figures significantly in the life of Jesus.

In the past, this last connection was bad news for Jews. It generated the so-called blood libel, alleging that a Christian boy's blood has to be mixed into the dough for the matzot ritually prepared for Passover. Wherever the blood libel was promulgated, it would generate pogroms where we Jews would be killed and our houses pillaged.

Thank God, blood libel stories have faded from the American scene, and the connecting link between Easter and Passover has taken on an increasingly positive cast. Jews are inviting Christian friends to their Seder, the traditional Jewish home celebration that occurs on Passover, much as Christians invite Jews to join in Easter egg hunts.

Then, I heard of a new development—Seders devised by Christians to help celebrate Maundy Thursday. The word "Maundy" comes from the Latin word *mandatum,* which gave us the English word for "mandate" and "command"; it refers to the *command* to love one another that Jesus gave to his disciples at the Last Supper. This sounds a lot like the mandate I received at the Cathedral.

Maundy Thursday commemorates the last regular day in the life of Jesus, ending with the Last Supper, which in fact was a Seder. That link seemed to me at first to provide an excellent basis for a truly ecumenic celebration.

I was pleased to be invited to join a Maundy Thursday Seder in the spring of 1997. The event was sponsored by St. Mark's on the Hill, an Episcopal congregation in Pikesville, Maryland, a heavily Jewish suburb of Baltimore. The Reverend Robert H. Stucky, rector of Saint Mark's, who led the event, had prepared a special guidebook based on the *Haggadah,* the standard Jewish text for conducting a Seder.

Father Stucky stressed his intention to create a truly ecumenical service. In a briefing before the event, he said:

We first began this Seder on a small scale with 30 people, or so. Many who attended were Jewish friends dissatisfied with their own experiences of the Seder. From the menu to the time frame to the Haggadah particulars, everyone had input as to how best to celebrate it in this community. The primary translation of the Haggadah used was done by my Hebrew professor at Yale.

The original participants here at St. Mark's included a number of Christian-Jewish families seeking a way to bridge the two cultures and the gaps that had been reinforced by both Church and Synagogue. Our first Seder was so successful that it simply expanded by word of mouth, attracting nearly as many Jews as Christians.

The reality is that for many people, experientially it is still a revelation to realize that Jesus was not only Jewish, but considered a rabbi by his followers. Grasping that context sheds light on what he may have understood himself to be doing at the Last Supper, as distinct from what others have retroactively interpreted him to have done.

The integrity of the Haggadah [Seder ritual] speaks for itself, and its ceremonies and rituals will be duly performed with all the joy they are intended to convey. . . . Our intention is to maintain the integrity of both traditions without presenting either the Seder or the Eucharist as a hybrid of the other.

A day or two after the Maundy Thursday Seder, I sat down with Father Stucky to review the event, and he asked me how it landed for me personally.

"With all due respect, Father Stucky," I said, "for me, it had the quality of a Readers Digest story. Traditional Seders I've attended started at sundown and ended long after midnight. Your Seder was over in two hours, which felt rushed to me."

"I know," Father Stucky replied, "but remember that the event falls right in the middle of Holy Week, a week of our most extensive and daily religious ceremonies. I didn't want to overtax my parishioners. I don't want an extra celebration that makes the whole week's observances become too burdensome."

Father Stucky noticed my hesitation to say more; I didn't want to seem unappreciative.

"Speak your truth," he admonished. "I really want to hear your reactions."

"Well, again speaking personally," I said, "I missed the silly songs we sang and the familiar games we played at the Seders of my uncle Max."

"I get what you mean," Father Stucky said. "Silly songs and games would be unfamiliar to the non-Jews present, and they would distract from the primary purpose of our observation and its relation to the events of Holy Week."

"Yes, let's compare the overall purpose of the two holidays. Speaking broadly, are the two comparable?" I asked.

"A good question," Father Stucky said. "The issue goes both ways. Some of the Christians present may not have grasped the full significance of the Seder as a celebration of slaves in Egypt celebrating their freedom from bondage. However, it is no less probable that some of the Jews present failed to grasp the profound symbolism of Jesus' actions in the Jewish context of Christian theology."

I wanted to stay grateful for having been invited, so I emphasized to Father Stucky that I found a lot to like in his Maundy Thursday Seder. I mentioned that his Haggadah was tailored with loving attention to both Christians and Jews, and the meal had authentic Jewish recipes that rivaled any prepared in Jewish homes.

In the final analysis, however, the Maundy Thursday just didn't satisfy me as a joint celebration. Inescapably, it was a hybrid, and the allure of hybrids is misleading. If you were a beef producer, and you'd cross one of your cows with a dairy breed, you'd expect the hybrid to produce more milk for its calves. Similarly, if you were a dairyman and you'd cross one of your cows with a beef bull, you'd expect to have more meat to sell from the resulting calf.

That's actually true, but there would be no net gain. Purebred milk cows outproduce the dual-purpose cows by a long shot in milk yield, and purebred beef cattle consistently outproduce the dual-purpose cattle in meat yield.

Similarly, you'd expect a Maundy Thursday to bring the best of

Easter and of Passover to a joint celebration. Actually, it dilutes the spirit of both. Also, it unveils the shift in symbology that occurred after Proto-Christians split off from traditional Judaism. You're reminded that the matzot at Passover are called "the bread of affliction," but when transposed into Christian practice, they became wafers to represent the body that Christ offered up for the salvation of man.

I can't help but conclude that much of the significance of each "pure" celebration gets lost in a "hybrid" fusing the two of them. Traditions in their full richness can be transmitted with full benefits only in separate ceremonies.

Trying to Meet Halfway

I am a persistent sort, and I kept looking for ways that Jews and Christians can meet somewhere in the middle. When I heard that messianic Jews, popularly known as "Jews for Jesus," had devised a service to include both Jews and Christians, I decided to check it out one fine Sabbath morning.

The Rosh Pina Congregation is located in Owings Mills, Maryland, an upscale, heavily Jewish Baltimore suburb. I sat down in the back of the sanctuary and observed.

The service offered a fair mix of Judaic and Christian practice. The Jewish references were many, and the ritual symbols, like prayer shawls and skullcaps, gave the prayer hall a Jewish tone. There was even a flag of the State of Israel up front.

Still, the service was recognizably Christian. The sermon and Bible readings both derived solely from the New Testament.

So, does messianic Judaism work?

I meditated on this extensively. Not surprisingly, my musings focused heavily on the originality of their inserting Jesus prominently into a Jewish religious ceremony. In an obvious nod to Jewish sensibilities, his name was transmuted into Joshua, the Anglicized version of his Hebrew name, Yehoshua. In other messianic groups, "Joshua" is further Judaized into "Yoshke." Either version works better for me than "Jesus" because the Jewish version of his name highlights the historical Jesus, not the theological Jesus.

I couldn't find anything un-Jewish in the teachings of Joshua recounted in the service. The historical Jesus was trained in Jewish lore, and direct quotes from his preachings can be traced to established Jewish sources.

So, why can't we all accede to a spectrum of belief? The question isn't new, and it was explored in depth by Amos Elon in the book *The Pity of It All,* which I mentioned earlier.

In a lengthy discussion (pages 208 and 227), Elon cites the German-Jewish theologian Hermann Cohen (1842–1918), who advocated merging Judaism and Christianity into one all-encompassing faith. Dr. Cohen even acceded to shifting the Sabbath from Saturday to Sunday. He said, "Jews must be masters of the Sabbath, not its slaves." Assimilation attained a higher value than tradition.

His contemporary Rabbi Wilhelm Klemperer even composed a bedtime prayer for his young sons that exemplified Dr. Cohen's Unitarian principle: "I trust in God and His embrace; in His mercy and good grace." It was a variant of the standard Protestant couplet, "I trust in God and His embrace; in Christ's blood and His good grace."

The desire for an "all-encompassing faith" continued, for example in the "theosophy movement" that started in Europe around the turn of the nineteenth century. This movement tried to encompass all philosophies centered on a belief in God. The theosophy movement soon split, with the departing group, called anthroposophy, wishing to pray without any reference to God. Instead they wanted to express their reverence to nature. I was a fellow traveler with the anthroposophists for a while and I learned their Grace Before Meals, which illustrates their approach. I wish I could sing it to you, but just the words need to suffice:

115

Grace Before Meals
Earth who gave us all this food!
Sun who made it ripe and good!
Dearest Sun and dearest Earth,
We will not forget your worth.

Since God governs both Earth and Sun, perhaps even we God-centered philosophers can use such an invocation to march in unison toward my Vision of Love.

I also tried to visualize a rainbow of beliefs that both Christians and Jews could claim a part of. Its bright red hue on one margin represents the fervent devotion to Jesus that fundamentalist Christians exhibit; its middle, centered on the green, suits the more liberal elements of Christianity; and the far margin, shimmering in purple, represents broad-minded Jews who respect the historical "Joshua."

Messianics seem to attract "purple" Jews. I heard this expressed by Marta Thomassen, a member of the messianic Jewish congregation of Amsterdam, in the Netherlands. Born Jewish, she now belongs to a mixed family of Christians and Jews, and she seems perfectly comfortable in an environment that fits Jesus into a Jewish observance. She expressed that clearly in an email she sent me:

> I feel at home in this Messianic synagogue because we have found a ground and an anchor in the Torah and its Mitzvot (commandments). Our belief that Joshua is the Messiah is not principally expressed by evangelizing—I see that as a most useless activity. Whether people believe Jesus is the Messiah is not as relevant as getting to know Adonai and studying Torah.
>
> In spite of what a lot of Christians and Liberals think, we consider ourselves truly Jewish and not a branch of some Christian church. I see it as being like Joshua's first congregation—Orthodox in orientation but modern in the sense of being relevant to the present day!

Actually, we consider mainstream Christianity in its current form as false Torah. We can't see, for example, why they shifted the Shabbat to Sunday and did away with the Jewish holy days.

However, we don't focus much on belief or worship in the traditional sense. Our worship is dancing Davidian dances, reading and sharing ideas afterwards, and encouraging each other in leading a productive life.

Marta realizes that her group goes against the flow of mainstream Judaism, which views the messianic movement as a Trojan horse to lure gullible Jews into converting. I can see why Jewish leaders think that way, even by just considering the name of the messianic church I visited in Baltimore. Rosh Pina is a biblical metaphor. It comes from a psalm describing a once-rejected stone that later was honored by being chosen as the cornerstone of some fancied building (Psalm 118:22).

This Old-Testament imagery in the name and a big Star of David on the exterior give Rosh Pina Congregation the appearance of a truly Jewish place of worship. Even Christian voices have taken issue with that rather deceptive approach.

For example, let me quote the Reverend Frank Eiklor, who heads an outreach organization called Shalom International and who regularly sends me his newsletters. In the issue of December 1, 2007, he wrote, "I sense the need for Christian integrity in order to avoid even the appearance of deceit. That's why I tell my messianic friends . . . that if they are to be denounced by . . . Jews for believing in Jesus, let it be out front—no disguise or deceit. Put the word 'messianic' on the sign outside of the building, so no one can say, 'They are trapping innocent Jews who don't know who they are.'"

However, I didn't want to discount the Rosh Pina congregation just for its name and its insignia. I wanted to look deeper, to see how "Jews for Jesus" could be a model for Christian-Jewish accommodation. In the end, it didn't work for me, mainly because Jesus is so central to Christian worship. Neither the messianics, who squeeze Joshua into Jewish services, nor Rabbi Klemperer, who squeezed Jesus altogether out of his "unitarian" prayer, pay their dues to Jesus' centrality.

If I were to select a theme in Jewish liturgy repeated as often and fervently as Jesus is in Christian worship, I'd pick the Sabbath, which Dr. Cohen tried to shift from Saturday to Sunday. Just as belief in Jesus sustains the Christian, the paradise on earth offered by the traditional Saturday Sabbath sustains the Jew. We say, "More than the Jews have preserved the Sabbath, the Sabbath has preserved the Jews." The sustenance of both Jesus and the Sabbath are valid in their own environment. Mixing the environments dilutes their sustenance.

On the other hand, a joint celebration of faith for Jews and Christians still sounds so appealing. Why can't we be true Judeo-Christians, one in spirit and one in brotherhood? Why do we need to get hung up on the issue of the divinity of Jesus?

To get my head straight about this, I consulted Rabbi Lobb, with whom I discuss my religious quandaries. Rabbi Lobb answered me by stages.

- Stage one is that a practicing Jew can accede to the belief that Jesus once lived.

- Stage two is that a liberal Jew can even agree that Jesus was an influential rabbi in his time and appreciate that his words have made a crucial difference in the lives of millions.

- However, we are stuck at stage three: having to agree that Jesus was, is, or has become a unique or special part of God above and beyond what any holy person might achieve. Judaism teaches that we are **all** children of God. Furthermore, stage three is especially difficult to hurdle regarding statuary in a worship space. Judaism was formed in the crucible of a revolt against idol worship. Christian religions also reject idol worship in principle, but Catholic leaders, in the heat of attracting converts, gave in on the issue of statuary, as long as the sculpture represents Jesus, Mary, or the Saints.

Now, I can accede to seeing God's two faces, just as Kabbalists talk about the *Shechinah,* the feminine, loving, approachable aspect of God, as contrasted with *Adonai,* the less approachable, awe-inspiring aspect of God. We speak to the *Shechinah* as a "side" of God that seems more approachable and to *Adonai,* the side that seems distant and unapproachable. It is like calling our human parent "Father" when speaking of him deferentially, and "Daddy" when we speak to him affectionately.

If Christians see God as a Trinity, it could be along the same principle:

- One face is "The Father," who watches caringly over us like a human father guarding his children.

- The second face, "The Son," is the inspirational aspect of God, the moving force which inspires prophets and generates visions (like my Vision of Love).

- The third face, "The Holy Ghost," represents *Adonai,* the unapproachable, awe-inspiring face of God.

In another way of looking at the issue, I can gravitate to a position called *radical monism,* which holds that *Creator and Creature and Everything Else* is "All One." (This concept is presented in clear detail by Rabbi Lawrence Kushner's book, *The Way into Jewish Mystical Tradition,* Jewish Lights Publishing, 2001, pp. 25–26.) If everything and anything is all God, then it doesn't matter if one of the Everythings is The Father, The Son, or the Holy Ghost! When I examine these aspects of Stage 3, I consistently speak about God as the same person. By contrast, I cannot **agree** to praying to three separate, individual, independently acting members of a Trinity.

What makes the Christian view of God absolutely unacceptable for me are:

- The Jewish concept of a Unitary God,

- The watchword of my Jewish faith, "God is One," and

- The Jewish abjuration of any intermediary between me and God.

Logically, I have fewer problems accepting the miraculous birth of Jesus, his special connection to God, and his sacrificial death. Actually, these key features of Jesus' life story parallel those of Isaac, the second Patriarch, as described in Torah.

Supernatural beings announce the imminent arrival of baby Isaac under extraordinary conditions. God overtly invests young Isaac with unprecedented power—the power to found a nation especially beloved by God. And then, inexplicably, God tells Papa Abraham to slaughter this Lamb of God.

Isaac, like Jesus, accepts his doom with apparent equanimity. Some versions of this legend—for example, in Muslim scripture—have him actually killed. But since the rabbis are troubled by resurrection stories, the official version is that Isaac was saved, moments before his execution, by the miraculous appearance of a Substitute Lamb, which gets the ax instead.

Morally, however, the two stories are identical: God kills his elect. Both stories almost force us to ask tough questions about God. However, for the purpose of this discussion, the key difference is that Isaac never is elevated from being a Patriarch to be a part of God, and neither do we pray to him.

So Jews, meaning to be ecumenical, might accede to a belief that Jesus was a man honored with a miraculous birth and condemned to a horrid death. To Christians who want Jews to believe in the divinity of Jesus, that wouldn't be good enough.

Nonetheless, we Jews can have many reasoned and reasonable discussion with Christians without having the divinity of Jesus be a stumbling block. We can discuss why we respond so viscerally to the notion that God kills his elect. We can even discuss why a "good" God permits evil to operate in his world, including such absolute horrors as a Holocaust that kills millions.

After all that musing about religious differences, I want to stop being so cerebral and just return to visualizing God's overarching love for all of humanity. We can actualize my Vision of Love between Christians and Jews even without achieving a "rainbow of common religions."

9.
Exploring Common Paths

E ven though I never found, or could devise, a worship service that fully satisfies both Jews and Christians, there is much we can do together. We can pray for each other, even with each other, each in his or her own way.

We don't travel the same highway, but we can stay close in pursuing similar goals. Our religious travels encounter similar obstacles, and working together can help us find a way around these obstacles.

Confronting Sexual Misconduct

In this context, the issue of sexual misconduct among clergy immediately comes to mind. It's a human problem, not limited to any faith community.

There is no doubt that the closeness and intimacy of religious experience and practice awakens sexual longing. The pleasure centers in the brain for spiritual ecstasy and sexual joy lie side by side, and these feelings can easily cross over.

Sometimes the crossover supports spirituality. For example, Catholic nuns get wedding rings, betrothing them to God, when they take vows committing them to their order. The nuns thus feel as committed to their "union" as couples that take on matrimony in church and synagogue.

Other times, the crossover leads to trouble—even horrifying trouble. The book *The Rabbi and the Hit Man: A True Tale of*

Murder, Passion, and Shattered Faith, written by my friend Arthur J. Magida, concerns Rabbi Fred J. Neulander, a popular clergyman who led a large temple in Cherry Hill, New Jersey, while conducting at least two extramarital affairs. In his case, he tried to cover up his missteps by arranging the murder of his own wife in 1994.

We can easily be lulled into condemning sexual misconduct and then just dismissing it. We would be better served to take a hard look at the process that gives rise to this behavior and see what can be done to stem it.

We need to openly admit to the seductive feelings that can arise from communing spiritually, especially in a setting that puts a man and a woman close together. This challenge gets exacerbated when the man (or the woman) is the charismatic leader of a spiritual community. Merging into the arms of a spiritual leader can be extremely comforting, particularly if the congregant is in a vulnerable emotional state.

I don't know at what point third parties should intervene in such a relationship. Orthodox Jews set up extremely strong and absolute barriers. They seat men and women separately during services and even prevent eye contact between them by a *mechitzah,* a physical and visual barrier. Women may not sing aloud in an assembly with men, to keep from arousing sexual excitement. And no man, not even a rabbi, may set up a meeting with a woman (other than his wife) without others being present.

To me, these restrictions seem a bit extreme, but they show an approach that people interested in the challenge can investigate further. ALEPH, the umbrella organization of the Jewish Renewal movement to which I belong, has had a long-standing ethics policy summarized in the "Procedure Regarding Breach of Professional Trust: Sexual and Financial Ethics."

This is a noble document, but in practice, it did not serve to restrain a well-known and popular author and teacher who turned out to be a predatory male. We had hired him to teach two one-week classes before we heard first-person testimony alleging sexual abuse at another venue. When we discovered that the teacher also had lied and deceived his way into our tent, we permanently banned him from our community.

Sunny Schnitzer, spiritual leader of the Bethesda, Maryland, Jewish Congregation, a Jewish group that once sponsored the offending teacher, cited in the June 1, 2006, issue of the *Washington Jewish Week* "the pitfall of elevating a spiritual leader above his or her message." Schnitzer summed up the situation succinctly by saying, "Guruhood is a really toxic place when it's all about the teacher and not the teaching."

In response to this egregious case, the Jewish Renewal movement launched another round of toughening and tightening our ethics policy. However, even the strictest policy provides no absolute guarantee against wrongdoing, and habitual offenders like the one we encountered present a truly complex problem. A friend close to the case explained why in a personal communication:

> In trying to deal with this problem, ALEPH consulted with legal, ethical, law enforcement, and forensic authorities covering not only sexual abuse but also substance abuse. From them, we learned that serial offenders are deeply compelled and sick human beings. The prognosis for a "cure" is almost nil. Recidivism rates are astronomical.
>
> The best that can be hoped for is in-patient therapy followed by close monitoring and lifetime participation in a program similar to Alcoholics Anonymous, where the person acknowledges the sickness, submits to close monitoring, and avoids any temptation to slide back. This includes safeguards to prevent a habitually sexually abusive spiritual leader from ever again serving as a teacher or clergy.

The offending teacher who slipped through our system supports my belief that predatory behavior is hard to regulate. Even though he publicly admitted his guilt in 2006, he is now saying it was all a big misunderstanding. He returned to the lecture circuit, reinventing himself as a wondrous guru.

Looking more broadly at sexual misbehavior, it's important to separate a habitual offense from a single, isolated misstep. It's tempting to say that a one-time slip shouldn't result in an everlasting mark of Cain on the forehead. In practice, however, it's extremely difficult to distinguish a one-time offender from a chronic one.

It isn't even easy to assess the propriety of a sexual relationship between a religious leader and a congregant, even if both are unmarried. This is recognized in the Jewish Renewal "Procedure" (cited above), which remarks:

> Although not automatically unethical, any sexual relationship between a single clergy person and a single congregant is fraught with risks for both parties and is illegal in some states. These risks include ambiguities about the perceived power of the clergy, the clergy person's ability to provide future pastoral care for the congregant, and the future of both parties in the congregation.

Whatever their religious affiliation, institutions need to give high priority to protecting themselves against misconduct by clergy. They must find a way to see the gradated difference between a sincere (but risky) relationship, a one-time sexual misstep, and a habitual offense.

Furthermore, they must find a way to avoid unfairly accusing clergy of sexual misconduct. This aspect of the problem was so graphically illustrated in the 2008 movie *Doubt,* with Meryl Streep, Philip Seymour Hoffman, and Amy Adams.

I worked out three bare-boned suggestions for how an institution can go about preventing sexual harassment without slipping into a false accusation. Here is my three-part outline:

• First, weave a protective net for vulnerable potential victims.

- Second, once allegations of an offense occur, develop effective yet discreet procedures for getting at the truth. These procedures certainly should protect teachers and clergy against false charges that could ruin a good reputation undeservedly.

- Third, if an allegation proves factual, establish standards to deal with the offender and to provide appropriate restitution to the victim; both might benefit from being directed to psychological counseling.

That outline is just my idea; hopefully it can help in developing guidelines that suit our faith communities. Communities could cooperate and coordinate this work, and the resulting policy could be the same or similar for all involved.

The Role of Women in Faith Communities

A second, important consideration for faith communities concerns the role of women in faith communities. Traditionally, both Christians and Jews have accepted the gender inequality that permeates Scripture. That attitude is changing, as part of a movement in the general society to eliminate gender inequality. Even ordination of women has become commonplace in many Christian and Jewish faith communities.

The Roman Catholics and Orthodox Jewish communities have resisted this change, but even there, the dominance of men is starting to fray at the edges. While most Catholics say they think the church will change its teaching on the use of contraceptives by 2050, fewer than half believe that the Catholic Church will allow priests to marry or women to be ordained, according to a poll by the Pew Research Center in 2015, titled "U.S. Catholics Open to Non-Traditional Families."

My friend Joy Smith strongly supports ordination of women or at least a more active role in the Roman Catholic hierarchy. She has risen as high as a woman currently can, and she doesn't think that's enough. When we discussed the topic, she wrote:

> I think that the Church tripped during the centuries when they tried to codify and absorb 'traditions' pertaining back to Mary, holding that she was undoubtedly free of sin—beyond what is attainable by other human beings. This concept came from St. Augustine, who said: 'All men are sinners, except the Holy Virgin Mary . . .' [De nat. et grat. 36, 42]. The Church essentially put the person of Mary in a position that is impossible for any woman to attain.
>
> Why did the Church go that route? Why did they open the door for women to feel less than holy because they had intercourse with their husbands? Why is a nun more holy and even given the title 'religious' because she vowed to abstain from intercourse? Does this not say something about prejudice in the Church against women?

I doubt whether any Church authority will ever directly answer Joy's poignant question, but her role as Chaplain in itself shows the restrictions on women's participation are lessening.

In the Jewish world, the tide of ordaining women ebbs and flows. In a moment of ebb-tide, the Orthodox Union of Congregations in the United States, after a year of discussion, reaffirmed its position in 2018, disallowing women rabbis. At the same time, they left the door open for the next three years to member congregations who in fact have hired women rabbis. Squirming past this anomaly, Allen Fagin, executive vice president, commented, "[I have] hopes that they will modify their practices so they will come into compliance with the responses of the rabbinic [review] panel . . .. Our fervent hope is that they will come into conformity [within three years]."

Countered Rabbi Shmuel Herzfeld, spiritual leader of the Orthodox Ohev Sholom Congregation in Washington, DC, "[My own prayer] is that in these three years, the [decision] will be reevaluated, that there will be new leadership that will not be so narrow-minded and shortsighted; and that [we] can grow and be a more and more open and inclusive organization."

Rabbi Steven Pruzansky, who leads Orthodox Congregation B'nai Yeshuron in Teaneck, New Jersey, added that "the Jewish people lose when we cannot in a formal way access the talents and brains of half our population. The survival of the oral tradition requires that past and future merge in the present. We are at an inflection point with this new movement [toward female clergy]." (Quotes published in the Florida Jewish Journal, Feb. 7, 2018.)

Explained David Hartman of the Shalom Hartman Institute of Jerusalem as far back as 2008, "We think the title 'rabbi' is important because in the Jewish tradition, the highest level of educator was given the title rabbi, which literally means *teacher*. Today, the top-tier [women] educators seek the title of *rabbi* to reflect their status as well." (Published in the Jerusalem Post of January 10, 2008.)

Some women prominent in the Orthodox world, on the other hand, see that desire for status in a different light. Feige Twerski, the wife of an Orthodox rabbi, presented her opposition with a simple question mark in the title of her article, "A Women's Place Is . . . at the Pulpit?" which appeared in *Ami Living* magazine, June 1, 2011, on page 49. She wrote:

> There is [no] question about a woman's ability and competence to do anything she chooses to undertake. Equality from a Torah perspective should be seen as meaning 'of equal importance,' rather than 'the same.'
>
> As people of faith, we firmly believe in a purposeful Creator, the only One who has a clear vision of mankind's destiny. As such, He created two genders, male and female. He did so precisely because each gender's charge and mission is distinct and unique.

Jewish and Christian communities can help each other in dealing with gender issues, but we need to do so with tact and understanding. This came to the fore during the clash between a Jewish and a Catholic community in St. Louis. Fox News, in their telecast of October 10, 2007, explained how the Jewish community became involved:

> The Central Reform Congregation offered its synagogue for Sunday's ordination of two women . . . who profess to be Roman Catholic—Rose Marie Dunn Hudson, 67, of Festus, and Elsie Hainz McGrath, 69, of St. Louis. [They] are to be ordained by a former nun as part of Roman Catholic Women-priests, a small movement that began in 2002 independently from the Roman Catholic Church.
>
> The Reform congregation's rabbi, Susan Talve, informed her friend and colleague, the Rev. Vincent Heier, who directs the archdiocese Office for Ecumenical and Inter-religious affairs, of the decision.
>
> Heier told her it was unacceptable.
>
> "It's not appropriate to invite this group, to aid and abet a group like this, which undercuts our theology and teaching," Heier said he told Talve.
>
> Rabbi Talve did it anyway and the Rev. Heier cut off all further relations with her.

Major players in the interfaith movement weighed in on the issue. One such vocal voice belongs to Rosann Catalano, a Roman Catholic scholar and associate director of the Institute for Christian and Jewish Studies in Baltimore.

She commented, "Whether the decision [by Rabbi Talve] was proper and wise depends on what your priority is. If it's interfaith relations, the answer is probably no. If it's sanctuary and hospitality, maybe you do that, realizing you will have to pay a price."

In conclusion, Rosemary Catalano echoed Feige Twersky when

she asked, "Is it possible the Holy Spirit is speaking through the faithful? I raise the question."

I also raise the question without having an answer at the ready. In truth, I see value in gender roles in religious practice. For example, I would like to have the opportunity open to Catholics who can meet their religious leader in a confession booth and, in spiritual closeness, say, "Father, I have sinned." Absolution from a father figure to me seems emotionally healthy. Just as the family has developed important gender-specific roles, so have the church and synagogue.

Wherever we find ourselves in this discussion, we can't close our eyes and ears to women who plead forcefully and passionately for greater participation, like the two Catholic women in St. Louis. I think our faith communities can help each other with this issue, but we need to avoid the friction that happened in St. Louis.

Cooperating on Social and Environmental Issues

A third issue on which Jews and Christians can effectively work together involves social and environmental issues. A major theme of Judaism is the impulse to repair the world, or at least keep it from falling apart. This impulse is known in Hebrew as *tikkun olam,* first described by fifteenth-century Jewish kabbalists as an effort to repair mystical elements that were broken and shattered during creation.

Later sages have applied *tikkun olam* to social action, saying that God purposely didn't make the world perfect so that we, as partners, have a chance to strive for perfection. They termed the work *gamilut chassadim*—"acts of human kindness." Kindness was ascribed to God, and humans reciprocating with kindness was seen as forming a man-God partnership.

Jewish thought brims with references to both terms. You can find *gamilut chassadim* mentioned even in song: "The world is supported on three principles: On Torah, on worship, and on deeds of human kindness"; and you can find *Tikkun* even in journalism. It is the single-word name of a widely read Jewish monthly.

Similarly, Christians want to do more than just pray for a more perfect world. Many congregations work structurally, consistently, and intensively to achieve social justice, relieve suffering, and preserve the environment. This is a good arena for cooperative action by church and synagogue.

For example, my congregation in Florida, Temple Adath Or, and the local Catholic Diocese came together after the devastating earthquake that hit Haiti on January 12, 2010. My rabbi, Marc Labowitz, and our common friend, Bishop Michel Pugin, decided to help the Renmen Foundation, which operates in Haiti and has its Florida office in my hometown of Deerfield Beach. (The acronym "Renmen" stands for *Recuperation des Enfants Necessiteux et Mal Encadres,* which means Recuperation of Needy and Underprivileged Children.)

The two religious leaders chose Renmen because it had an established infrastructure in Haiti and was effectively helping children long before the earthquake. The two Florida congregations agreed to focus on a Renmen orphanage in La Plaine du Cul de Sac near Port au Prince, which was heavily affected by the disaster. We heard that the fifty-two children at the orphanage were threatened by exposure to the elements and diseases like malaria. First aid and other essential supplies were urgently needed.

Father Michel, who speaks fluent French and some Creole, the languages of Haiti, boarded the first airplane that would take him to the orphanage "to help restore some normalcy to the children's lives," as he said before he left. "This is what I was ordained to do, providing help and comfort to those who need it most. I can't tell you how excited I am that I'm going."

"Tell you what," Rabbi Labowitz said, "next time you go there, I'll organize a work detail to go with you."

Recruiting the volunteers raised the interest of both faith

communities—including the ones who couldn't go along to Haiti. The stay-at-homes assembled so many contributions, including mine, that we filled an entire shipping container!

The rabbi and the bishop assembled a sizable group to work at the Renmen orphanage. They helped cook for the kids, clear the land, and return the buildings to normal. Most importantly, Father Michel said, the two congregations supported the orphans emotionally. They needed love and care to overcome the anguish caused by the earthquake and its aftermath.

Building Houses While Tearing Down Prejudice

In my home town of Baltimore, Maryland, faith communities joined with the NGO *Habitat for Humanity* to build new homes and refurbish deteriorating houses for underprivileged people.

Community organizer Jayna Powell reported the genesis of this cooperative work in *Habitat World Magazine* (pages 6–7, March 2008). She said:

> Most *Habitat* affiliates had an existing organization in their city that did interfaith dialog with Christians, Jews, and Muslims. We didn't have one of those in Baltimore. So what I discovered was that we were going to have to design an organization of the three faiths that would both talk together and work together.
>
> When we designed it, we made it about much more than building houses. That's been the best part about this—that people just laugh together . . . with people that . . . wouldn't have worshiped in the same places . . . but they're together on an equal basis when they're working on this house.
>
> Once people hold Sheetrock for each other, they are more interested in sharing worship as well, or seeing how others worship. Even though everybody doesn't keep kosher, we decided some of them will, [so] let's find out what that means.

Participants learned that *kosher* and the Muslim's *halal* were quite similar, and all of them ate kosher snacks together at the building site.

Powell started with what she called "pre-build events." She encouraged leaders from the three faith communities to arrange a series of worship services in their home congregations. At mosques on Friday, synagogues on Saturday, and churches on Sunday, speakers explained the basics of the other faiths while Powell explained the building plans.

Building houses and building interfaith bridges worked well together.

Mourning Loved Ones with Compassion

The pain at "losing a loved one" is universal, and religious communities can lean on one another in ameliorating the loss. In its May 28, 2007 issue, *Newsweek* magazine explored this potential.

Jess Decourcy Hinds of Brooklyn, New York, wrote a "My Turn" article in which she presented the need for more supportive practice for people who grieve. She said, "Losing my father was painful enough without having other people try to talk me out of my grief. I resent the condolence cards that hurry me thorough my grief as if it were a dangerous street at night. Why don't people say 'I am sorry for your loss' anymore?"

Rabbi Julie Hilton Danan from Chico, California, responded in the June 11 issue, suggesting a Jewish way for relieving Hinds's complaint. She cited her own recent loss and said:

I was once again filled with gratitude for the ancient wisdom of the Jewish tradition, which provides a structured framework for grief. Mourners stay at home for a week while members of the community come to comfort them. Comforters are instructed to remain silent until the mourner speaks and to follow his or her emotional cues.

A full array of customs and traditions supports the mourner from the death and through the stages of grief, and makes remembrance a part of nearly every holiday season."

Dr. Simcha Paull Raphael, one of my teachers, has described these customs in touching detail in his book, *Jewish Views of the Afterlife* (Jason Aronson Publishers, 1996). I think it is well worth reading, not only by Christians struggling with the aftermath of death, but also by Jews who want to recapture some of the time-tested traditions of our people.

Many Western religious groups are also exploring Eastern traditions, which don't see death as "such a loss." Both Christians and Jews now examine whether there's more to life than birth, suffering, and death—we join each other in exploring whether our soul is eternal and life and death represent stages in an eternal Wheel of Life.

Finding comfort and consolation with each other are ideal ways to realize my Vision of Love.

10.
Facing the Challenge

Our society is at its most "Judeo-Christian" when it comes to marriage, but I have problems with this type of union. I surprise people when I say that in the same breath that promotes my Vision of Love between Christians and Jews.

My own worshipping community wouldn't have a problem if I intermarried; in fact, quite a few member couples in my religious group are themselves intermarried. Neither would my father have lectured me on intermarriage if he had had the chance—he died when I was eleven.

My father did tell me he was strongly attracted to a blonde Christian woman while he was in college, but he never considered marrying her. That bit of his history speaks much louder than a lecture.

Neither my father nor my two grandfathers were religiously observant, but none of them ever married out of the faith. My mother's father actually went to great length to preserve this tradition.

Grandfather Jakob Kramer lived with me and my parents when I was young, and his stories about life in the outback of South Africa excited my imagination. He told me that when he was of marriageable age, there were no unmarried Jewish women in the outback.

He solved his desire to marry a "nice Jewish girl" by having his brother scout one out for him back in their native Bavaria. His sort-of mail order bride came to live with him in the outback—that shows the length to which my family went to marry within the group.

Exploring Intermarriage

Joy once challenged me, saying: "If you felt yourself falling in love with a Christian, why wouldn't you consider marriage? You're so firm in your own religion. What's so threatening about living with someone who practices another?"

I formulated my reply with the song that opens the musical play *Fiddler on the Roof.* The title contains but a single word: "Tradition," and that is where I take my stand.

The musical is based on Sholem Aleichem's story of *Tevye, the Dairyman,* set in early nineteenth century Russia. The opening scene shows an actor sitting precariously on a rooftop while playing a fiddle. The image graphically demonstrates how hard it is for a traditional Jew to balance off the rapidly changing world outside against the traditions of his fathers.

The tension in the story arises because each of Tevye's three oldest daughters rebels against that tradition by means of her choice of a marriage partner.

Daughter Number One picks a poor, young tailor instead of the rich, old, crabby butcher her father had selected. Pappa is disappointed. She begs. Pappa relents, thinking up a strange midnight ruse to get Mamma to concur. And off the happy lovers go, to a life upstairs from the tailor's shop.

Daughter Number Two rebels more grandly by falling for a professional agitator, a Communist organizer. He's Jewish, but you can hardly tell by the irreligious talk he utters. Pappa is appalled. She begs. Pappa seeks a possible excuse for her. He convinces himself: Love! Reluctantly and sadly, he blesses her decision. And off the newlyweds go to exile in Siberia, a honeymoon site reserved for rebels by the Russian government.

Daughter Number Three really rebels—defiance beyond conception! Her beau's a well-connected Christian in the Russian village right next to the Jewish *shtetl* of Anatevka.

She begs Pappa to bless her choice also. He deliberates, "Well, he's kind-hearted, he's competent, he has good prospects, and . . . he's a Christian—never!"

There is nothing that can balance off that difference. "Marry that man," Tevye says out loud, "and by me, you're dead." She marries him anyway and moves to a manor house in the Christian village. In practice, said house was more remote than Siberia because the entire Jewish community shuns the new couple.

If you understand the pain in Tevye's decision, you also understand why wouldn't I marry a Christian. Along with Tevye, the dairyman, I painfully answer, "Tradition."

Well, maybe you still don't quite understand. We both know that I'm not tied to tradition as strongly as Tevye. I live in twenty-first-century America, not in nineteenth-century Russia.

Beyond tradition, I'm motivated by a desire to see the Jewish way of life continue into the future. Currently, about half of the Jews who marry choose Christian partners, so the Jewish population of America is being halved each generation. For Jews in America, to put it bluntly, intermarriage means oblivion.

This fear of attrition gets plenty of attention in the Jewish press. The February 2007 issue of *Hadassah Magazine* featured and article by Linda Brockman, about a talented congresswoman from Florida, Ileana Ros-Lehtinen. By Jewish law, she is Jewish, being born of a Jewish mother. Her mother's parents were Jews who came to Cuba from Turkey. However, Ileana's father was Roman Catholic, and her mom converted to his religion.

The congresswoman's own children still hear the echo of Judaism. For the article, the congresswoman said, "My daughters were baptized and confirmed, but part of their upbringing has been a celebration of their Jewish ancestry."

I don't doubt that the cultural diversity in the congresswoman's background has shaped who she is and has enlarged her horizons. Still, the intermarriage in her family has driven one of our best and brightest out of the fold. Future generations are unlikely to preserve the "pride in their grandmother's Jewish roots" that the congress-woman says her own daughters have maintained.

Overall, more than 80 percent of non-Jewish partners married to Jews remain in their former religion, as reported in the April 21, 2006, issue of the *Baltimore Jewish Times.* Their children obviously receive a mixed message. Even though a 2001 study suggests that two-thirds of intermarried families say that they raise their children Jewish, there is little evidence that these children become practicing Jews.

Statistics are notoriously impersonal, so let me explain how the issue of intermarriage has affected me personally. From my first two marriages, I had two children, a boy, Albert, and a girl, Liora. Both attended Hebrew school, but Jewish traditions didn't become central to their lives; both lived in a non-Jewish environment once they became independent.

Albert turned to professional sports, a career in which Jews are noticeably lacking, and Liora went to a high school in Switzerland, where the overall Jewish population is noticeably thin. So I had plenty of foreboding that they might not find a Jewish marriage partner.

Albert never married and died young. Liora stayed single until she was almost thirty. Then came the decisive phone call from Switzerland, "Daddy, I met the man I'm going to marry. But, Daddy, he isn't Jewish."

I made two trips to Switzerland that year to deal with that situation. In the process, I got to know the prospective groom, Edouard, quite well. He is open and expressive, a good storyteller. He knew many Jews and their rituals, since his mother lived with a longtime boyfriend who is Jewish. Edouard considered converting to please Liora. In the end, however, he found he couldn't do this and stay true to himself.

So I took a step into territory where Tevye couldn't go and extended my blessing to the engaged couple. However, my concerns about tradition continued once their first child was born. They gave him a Jewish-sounding name, Mael David, and they exposed him from babyhood to some Jewish rituals.

However, a core issue faced us after he was born: the question of whether he should be circumcised. Circumcision is the symbol that makes a boy Jewish, so the issue was decisive for the future of my progeny.

In our discussions, I explained how the issue affected me. They understood, but they had strong reservations. In the end, Mael remained uncircumcised, and I have to respect that, too. My children decide the future; I only represent the past.

The entire family into which Liora has married is accepting and loving, and we all get along swimmingly. However, I am faced with being the last Jew in my line, and that engenders a palpable sadness. I experienced what many Jews of my generation have experienced. Our Jewish children are melting into the Christian pot as quickly as an iceberg in a summer sea.

I trust that you now understand why I'm anxious about Jews intermarrying. You may worry that this anxiety would lead me to advocate a law to prevent intermarriage. Don't worry. Laws and sanctions can't bring about my Vision of Love.

Solving the Jewish Question

There are Christians in America today who feel uncomfortable, or worse, living with Jews. They can't find room for us. They say, "After all, when you come down to it, America is a Christian country, isn't it?"

You could ascribe this notion to ignorance, but not so fast. Serious candidates for president of the United States have expressed that mindset in unguarded moments, even though surely they come across as better informed when they are watching their p's and q's.

Take, for example, what Senator John McCain, told "Beliefnet" during the 2008 presidential campaign. When asked how he evaluates candidates for office, he replied, "I prefer someone who I know has a solid grounding in my faith" since "the Constitution established the United States as a Christian nation."

And here is how Mike Huckabee, another Republican candidate in the same race, had expressed himself before Southern Baptist preachers in 1998, "Government [doesn't] have the real answers . . . real answers lie in accepting Jesus Christ into our lives . . . I hope we . . . take this nation back for Christ."

The error in these statements was ably exposed by Pastor Oliver "Buzz" Thomas, a minister in the Southern Baptist Church (as published in an op-ed piece in USA Today on Oct. 15, 2007). He said:

Many of the nation's loudest religionists continue to assert that America is a Christian nation in some legal or constitutional sense. The language of the original Constitution itself suggests otherwise. The only reference to religion is tucked away in Article VI and reads: 'No religious test shall ever be required as a qualification to any office of public trust under the United States . . . .'

[W]hy would the framers of our Constitution [then also] . . . adopt a constitutional amendment declaring that the new federal government could "make no law respecting an establishment of religion?" Easy. The framers . . . had witnessed the blood shed by governments in the name of religion. Europe was nearly destroyed by it.

Was it because they were militant atheists? Hardly. James Madison, the primary architect of our Constitution, . . . even considered a career in the [Presbyterian] ministry before opting for politics . . . . [Furthermore, his contemporary,] prominent Virginian Baptist John Leland . . . declared: "The notion of a Christian commonwealth should be exploded forever. The fondness of magistrates to foster Christianity has done it more harm than all the persecutions ever did."

No one can attest to that sad situation better than we Jews. Over and over again, Christian societies in Europe invited us Jews in for our talents until they suddenly discovered that we were threatening their "Christian nation." Once that realization registered, persecutions followed.

The Founding Fathers of America recognized the danger in a pendulum that swings between tolerance and persecution. They knew that it could take a swing at any religion unpopular at the moment. Pastor Thomas implies that they insisted on separating church from state to stop the pendulum from swinging as it had in Europe.

The founders were aware of more than just dangers inherent in an established religion. They also sensed, I believe, that there are positive results when a nation encourages a variety of religious beliefs.

Even during the darkest age of medieval Europe, scholars in monasteries found value in Jewish texts. However, they hardly ever consulted any living Jews. Instead, they perused what often had become stale information. You need living Jews and a vibrant Jewish culture to give a meaningful measure of talent to the Nation's treasure house of ethical living.

Our numbers always have looked puny in proportion to the overall population. In 1654, when the first boatload of Jewish refugees landed in New York (it was then still called New Amsterdam), they numbered only twenty-three. More Jews trickled in slowly over the later decades until our numbers reached about two million in 1880. Between that date and the start of World War I in 1914, an additional two million Jewish refugees, principally from Eastern Europe, dramatically raised the total Jewish population to about 100 million, equaling about 3 percent of the total U.S. population.

During all this history, starting in 1654 and continuing until today, America provided Jewish refugees a safe haven. America's welcome helped thousands escape successfully from the Inquisition, and American troops closed down gas chambers our persecutors had established during the Holocaust.

However, somewhere in their psyche, many Christians in America still fostered the hostile attitude toward Jews that their ancestors brought with them from Europe. Things were at their worst in my home state of Maryland. Jews were barred from any public office and from the voting booth until 1825, some forty-nine years after Maryland ratified the U.S. Constitution. Even though some of the nation's Founding Fathers, such as Thomas Jefferson, John Quincy Adams, and James Madison, went on record decrying Maryland's policies, no one challenged them in the state's legislature for twenty-one years.

When the first challenge was introduced in 1797, opponents in the Maryland legislature formed what they called a "Christian ticket." Its leader, Benjamin Galloway, took no pains to soften his anti-Semitic rhetoric. He won election to the legislature in 1823 by a large margin, apparently in major part because of his virulent opposition to what was called the "Jew Bill." It took twenty-eight years of debate before the House of Delegates finally passed the "Jew Bill." It passed by a single vote (26 to 25, with twenty-nine legislators purposefully absent).

Slowly and grudgingly, Christian Americans made room for us, even though anti-Jewish sentiments continued to be uttered. When the Nazi atrocities became known after World War II ended, these anti-Jewish sentiments went underground. However, even today most people in the United States don't realize that variety is America's strength. Yes, we have moved up the "acceptance ladder" from resentment to indifference to tolerance, but I believe it's high time that the Christian attitude move up another rung toward warm-hearted appreciation.

I would like Christians to promote true equality, without remnants of quotas and restrictions. I'd like to see Jews and Christians live happily together in neighborhoods they both care about and make more livable. And, in the churches, I am looking for content that makes loving and positive references and overtures to other religious groups.

In other words, I urge Christians to realize that Judaism matters, that it is an asset to America worth preserving. Once that happens, it will be clear that it requires action, not just theoretical assent to an ideal.

To preserve Judaism, stemming intermarriage ought to be high on the list of priorities. As I said earlier, we can't (and shouldn't) outlaw intermarriage or even inhibit it by community pressure as in Anatevka, in Tevye's Russia. We need to do it by attitude and by example.

Leaders in politics and public opinion should set the example. Unfortunately, this hasn't happened. As Rabbi Shmuley Boteach exclaimed in *Moment Magazine* in June 2000, "Why isn't there one Jewish figure as big as the Dalai Lama?"

Major families in public life have downplayed their Jewish background. Some felt the need to convert early, as was the case for the family of influential presidential candidate Barry Goldwater. His grandfather, Michel Goldwasser, came from Poland and stayed Jewish, but his father, Baron Goldwater, changed both his name and his religion, becoming an Episcopal.

Henry Kissinger, President Richard Nixon's quixotic alter ego, was born Jewish, and in his early life, he was religiously observant. As an early adult, he could have been considered a Jewish activist. He was one of the most effective Nazi hunters in the business after World War II ended.

However, as his fame grew, he distanced himself more and more from his Jewish background. His first wife, Ann Fleischer, was Jewish. His second wife, Nancy Maginnes, is not, which by itself says a lot.

When I contacted Kissinger about helping support Refusenik Jews in Russia, he didn't bother to answer. As far as I know, he never lifted a finger to help.

The only positive example I could find in our public arena is a U.S. Senator and a one-time candidate for the presidency, Joseph Lieberman. Both his former wife, Elizabeth Haas, and his current wife, Hadassah Lieberman, are Jewish. Even at the pinnacle of his public exposure, he maintained a confident participant in Jewish life. He obviously is aware of the issue I'm raising; he wrote the foreword to *Jews in American Politics* by Sandy Maisel, published by Rowman & Littlefield, 2001.

So I salute Senator Lieberman, openly Jewish, often questioned about it, and always ready with thoughtful responses. If other Jewish figures with high profiles were as forthright as Senator Lieberman and if Christian leaders encouraged them, the values of Jewish traditions might be saved for America's future. When it no longer is remarkable—and a challenge—for a Jew to be both active in politics and in his or her religion, then I think we'll have made a giant step forward toward my Vision of Love.

Exploring How the Messiah Will Come

I fervently long for the coming of the Messiah, a hope and expectation that many Christians and Jews have been praying for all along. Once a personage is recognized as the Messiah in this world, it wouldn't matter anymore whether he is Prophet, Savior, or even the Son of God. A true Messiah would embrace all of humankind.

I believe that *Tikkun Olam*, "repairing the world," hastens the arrival of the Messiah. However, instead of rolling up their sleeves and getting to work, as many congregations have done, others instead have spent fruitless hours on efforts to elevate an actual person to the level of Messiah. That's putting the cart before the horse, the way I see it.

People have stretched out their hands in peculiar ways to anoint some person the Messiah. For example, a Messiah appeared to some Christians in the person of Pastor José Luis de Jesús Miranda, who died in 2013, and to some Jews in the person of the Rabbi Menachem Mendel Schneerson, who died in 1994.

The rise of the Christian Messiah was reported in the February 5, 2007, issue of *Newsweek*. He led a Hispanic Evangelical sect called the Growing in Grace International Ministry, with headquarters in Doral, Florida. He declared himself the Messiah when Christ "integrated with him" in 1973. Over time, he declared himself the Second Coming of Christ.

As such, he rejected the continued worship of Jesus of Nazareth, and he decried the "lies of other churches," presumably because they didn't recognize him. Nonetheless, he commanded the loyalty of more than 100,000 followers in more than three hundred congregations in two dozen countries, from Argentina to Australia.

The elevation of Rabbi Menachem Mendel Schneerson also was gradual. Starting in 1951, he led the Lubavitcher Chasidim, who today constitute by far the largest Chasidic Jewish sect with probably double the worldwide membership of the José de Jesús group.

When some of Rabbi Schneerson's Chasidim first expressed the belief that he was the Messiah, he neither rejected nor supported this claim. However, he frequently spoke about the messianic age of peace, and until his death, he encouraged his followers to prepare for the coming of the Messiah.

When he died without having revealed himself as such, his closest advisers—the highest levels of Chabad's leadership—tried to put an end to the overt messianic fervor. That hasn't worked. Recently, one expert inside Chabad says that the majority of the movement still believes that the rebbe, alive or dead, is the Messiah.

Of course, events following the elevation of Luis de Jesus and Menachem Schneerson hardly support the claim that either one is the Messiah. Overall, the world hasn't improved significantly, and neither personage has gained the all-encompassing worldwide recognition we expect from a Messiah.

What are our prospects for experiencing the real coming? During a recent trip to Jerusalem, I gave that topic a lot of thought. When I visited friends and relatives in Israel, I found them surprisingly dispirited and hopeless.

I asked them about the prospects of peace, a solution to their problems with the Arabs. Their answer surprised me: "There is no solution." Apparently, they were wearied by recent, relatively insignificant, setbacks: Rockets fired by Arab fanatics from Gaza and bullets shot by Arab fanatics from the West Bank.

It seemed to me that the Israeli Jewish majority no longer believes that the acts of ordinary men can solve giant, intractable problems, and they seem to doubt that the Messiah will come to bring peace to the world. They were unable to see any light at the end of the tunnel.

That surprises me. I always have considered Israelis to be optimists. I admire their can-do spirit, their conviction that the Jewish State is an unshakable verity. The Israeli national anthem is "The Hope," and hope has been the Israelis' watchword.

So, why this hopelessness, this resigned acceptance of the status quo? After all, the prospect of the coming of the Messiah even gave hope to prisoners of the Holocaust. On their way to death in the gas chambers, they sang the stanza affirming the Messiah found in *Ani Ma-amin* (I Believe), the 13 Principles of the Jewish Faith composed by the famous Rabbi Moses ben Maimon (Maimonides) in the twelfth century. The lyrics proclaim:

Ani Ma-Amin

I believe with perfect faith in the coming of the Messiah.
Though he tarry, I remain steadfast in my belief
That the world will ultimately be redeemed.
I believe, totally, in the coming of the Messiah.
I remain steadfast, even though he is late.
Despite everything, I hope and trust.

I sing that song on the Sabbath, so obviously I share the faith it expresses, but I don't know how any candidate for Messiah would go about establishing his credentials. We hardly can expect that one day we'll wake up and there'll be a big parade, led by a Messiah on a white horse, the way Jews of Eastern Europe visualized his arrival. Even if, as they said, we'd recognize him by a golden goblet that he carries in his right hand, I don't think he'd be convincing to parade watchers today. Even if he materialized loaves and fishes in Bethesda, Maryland, as Jesus did near Bethesda in Judea, few of us skeptical Americans would be impressed enough to stop fighting and start loving one another.

The messianic age will happen when people are ready for it. A sense that things can't get any worse could put us in the proper frame of mind.

I think that this is exactly what happened when Jesus Christ appeared on the scene two thousand years ago. Things in Jerusalem had deteriorated to the point that any change advocated by a popular leader would be an improvement over what was going on. People flocked to Jesus out of a desperate hope for a better future.

Rather than looking for a true-blue Messiah today, I think we'd had better work and pray for a charismatic human leader —someone of real stature—who can lead our crazy world toward important objectives, like relieving global warming. I don't think that this savior will be a political leader. I see him more as a person with an elevated moral stature in the community, like Martin Luther King Jr. Whether we will actually bestow the title Messiah on that leader doesn't matter so much to me, as long as the person had the ability and charisma to usher us into the messianic age.

If a future leader actually does try to sell himself as the Messiah, it will be hard for him to establish his credentials. Even canonized Jewish lore does not provide a clear means of identification. We just are told that Elijah the Prophet will come to announce him and that he himself will show up as announced.

Trouble is, we'd have as difficult a time identifying Elijah as pinpointing the Messiah himself. Elijah has been dead these thousands of years and no one remembers what he looked like.

The New Testament doesn't give us many more clues than the older covenants. It speaks of John the Baptist as Elijah returned, but gives few descriptions. It's going to have to be a matter of faith, circumstance, or both that will reveal the Messiah to us.

Secular thinkers express similar hopes. In introducing the 2007 report of the Institute of Noetic Science, its president, James O'Dea, writes:

> This report is about [a] wholesale change from an unsustainable way of life—mired in the contradictions of dogmatic religion and secular political power and fueled by rampant profiteering and the coercion of science—to one in which both science and spirituality reconfigure our most basic understandings of human consciousness and how to live harmoniously in a healthy and sustainable ecosphere . . . . Transformation can begin with a small but significant shift in perspective that can precipitate whole-scale change.
>
> When the Age of Aquarius was announced in the 1960s, people already expressed this hope. Unfortunately, we haven't realized it yet.

Like Mr. O'Dea, I also look for change to come through a small but significant shift away from the strife and mistrust I saw in Jerusalem. The situation there begs for a change in our hearts and actions, and essentially that's what Jesus was trying to achieve.

Whoever Jesus was, I see him as a messenger intending to spread love and to inspire people to deal with one another more kindly. That's the type of Messiah I can warm to.

I don't expect to meet the Messiah on the road, with or without white horse and golden beaker. I think we will have to come to him, not vice versa. We can do that by sharing both the love of God and the love of Jerusalem with one another. When the fleece before our eyes finally falls away, and we fully realize that Arabs, Jews, and Christians all truly love Jerusalem, we'll find a peaceful way to share it.

Speaking even more universally, when we all work together for the well-being of humankind and emulate God's love by being loving to one another, that will be my sign that the Messiah has come. I hope and pray that I will see it happen in my lifetime. Nothing else can do more toward realizing my Vision of Love.

How Jews Seem Different

You can judge how close and comfortable Christians and Jews feel with each other by where they prefer to live. In my hometown of Baltimore, it's easy to see remnants of a ghetto mentality that pretty much keeps the two faith communities apart.

According to the 1999 demographic survey that I mentioned earlier, about 70 percent of Baltimore's 36,000 Jewish households lived in three general neighborhoods. Most typical is the Baltimore suburb of Pikesville and surroundings, where my late wife, Shana, and her two married daughters lived in the year 2000 when Shana and I got married.

Sure, like all immigrant groups, especially in the early generations after their arrival, Jews feel most comfortable living near and interacting with one another. However, I think our immigrant mentality also has persisted because Christians make us uncomfortable if we live in their neighborhoods. This discomfort doesn't mainly speak of intolerance as much as a harder-to-define impatience and suspicion.

I experienced this firsthand when I got my first job after completing graduate school in 1960. The job was in Cincinnati. It paid poorly, and my wife and I took an apartment in a low-rent, non-Jewish neighborhood.

When we moved in, I had a serious case of athlete's foot, and my podiatrist recommended soaking my feet in potassium permanganate. This treatment temporarily left the treated skin quite brown. On my way to the swimming pool, one of the neighbors stopped me. Pointing to my brown feet, she asked shyly, "Do all Jews have black feet?" Perhaps she was somewhat more comfortable with Jews that have only ten percent black skin than with African-Americans who are one hundred percent black!

That we were considered outsiders, much the same as blacks, came out through another interaction. We struck up, over the months, a "Hello, how are you?" relationship with an older couple, which progressed to borrowing the proverbial cup of sugar. The neighbors reached retirement age, and we sensed they'd soon move.

Sure enough, one day the neighbor lady came to say goodbye, and of course we asked where they were going. With a big smile on her face as she was leaning against our door jamb, she replied, "We're moving back to West Virginia, where there are no Nigras and no Je—" She stopped herself, turned red in the face, and just waved goodbye.

I remember an even more extreme example of discomfort with "Jews in our midst." I know a Jewish man who married a Christian girl, I think because she was a sexy blonde and because both wanted to spite their mothers. The mother of the groom was a literalist Orthodox Jew—a sour, controlling woman. I never met the Christian girl's mother, but by reputation she was hardly less tolerant of people outside her religious group and hardly more pleasant to be with.

What amazed me most about this marital experiment, was that the Christian girl would sling a string of anti-Semitic slurs at her husband whenever she got annoyed. Even though she had defied her mother, she had preserved her mothers hatred of Jews. In a way, her position as Jew-hater married to a Jew was perfect. She didn't have to step out of her front door to find a Jew to hate!

Perhaps this relationship stands for the attitude of many Christians toward Jews. They act nice when the weather is good but revert to anti-Semitism in foul weather.

My friend Fred Katz, the Holocaust survivor and sociologist whom I quoted earlier, has developed a sociological theory on this theme. He says:

> In good times, old animosities between tribes and faith communities seem to disappear. However, these animosities are like an underground stream.
>
> They keep flowing undetected until people tap into it again when they need someone to blame for a current misfortune.

Perhaps you think that limited personal horizons and ignorance led to the actions of my Cincinnati neighbors and the pretty Christian blonde who married a Jew. You could be right, but I still feel that Christians seem more comfortable when they can put some distance between themselves and us.

Often at work, I was the rare Jewish bird in the aviary. Coworkers seemed okay with my wearing a Star of David unobtrusively on a chain under my shirt. However, anything more obtrusive showing that my culture and religion differed from theirs seemed to make them uncomfortable.

In one job, where I think I was hired on purpose as the "token Jew," they soon got uncomfortable with their "experiment." No one said, "You're fired," but they suggested I might find better outlets for my talents and encouraged me to resign. I did. When I interviewed for another job, the company representative who acted as my host told me round-out that he doubted I'd be comfortable there. They were just not ready to work around a Jew.

In jobs where I felt comfortable to openly hang out as a Jew, conversations still made it clear that coworkers felt uncomfortable— not particularly with me, but with Jews that look too Jewish. My

Christian coworkers stared in disbelief at Orthodox Jewish men who wear black hats with broad brims, their earlocks dangling below. They wondered even more at women who eschewed the current sexy styles and wore long skirts and huge hats to cover their hair. Overtly or covertly, these Christian onlookers asked, "Can't Jewish objectives be achieved less flagrantly?"

I answer, "Yes, they can." The majority of Orthodox males don't stand out near as obviously. They wear relatively unobtrusive yarmulkes (skull caps) and don't dangle their earlocks. Their women wear street clothes that are modest but still look standard American.

So why do some Orthodox sects dress so in-your-face, like the Lubovicher Chasidim, a large group of observant Jews? They do so to honor their antecedents, a line of famous rabbinical leaders whose lineage started in Lubovich, Russia, in the eighteenth century.

It's a pretty simple explanation, but I wonder why I should have to present it. Why does it bother people more to see a Jew with long earlocks dressed in black than a Boy Scout with a crew cut dressed in khaki?

The website of the Boy Scouts of America explains quite clearly what the uniform signifies. It says, "The uniform makes the Boy Scout troop visible as a force for good and creates a positive youth image in the community. Boy Scouting is an action program, and wearing the uniform is an action that shows each Boy Scout's commitment to the aims and purposes of Scouting. The uniform gives the Boy Scout identity in a world brotherhood of youth who believe in the same ideals."

I posit that the "uniform" of the Lubovichers operates in much the same way. It is visible as a force for good and creates a positive religious image in the community. The dress code shows each Chasid is committed to the aims and purposes of Lubovich. The "uniform" gives the Chasid identity in a world brotherhood that believes in the same ideals.

So I ask you, why can a Christian's view of the world accommodate the uniform of Boy Scouts better than that of Orthodox Jews? You tell me!

I myself am happy that the Chasidim dare to dress the way they do. In my youth, the Nazis forced me to wear a large yellow Jewish star on my outer clothes to make sure I stood out from the Christian crowd. I hated that.

Chasidim stand out voluntarily, proud of their religion and conviction. I like that a lot better. I would not take on a Chasidic dress code myself, but I hope that a future generation will let people proclaim openly and freely what they stand for without requiring excuses or explanations.

Another source of discomfort expressed by Christians derives from a "sad and resigned affect" that they notice in some Jews. I remember a quote I read, I forgot where that "psycho-culturally, Jews have patterns toward misery, complaining and negativity." There's a certain truth to this charge sometimes described as "Jewish neurosis." Philip Roth and Woody Allen have made entire careers out of laughing at this!

Given our history, this tendency isn't surprising and it isn't really funny. We Jews have faced incessant persecution in nearly every generation. When persecutions skipped a generation, the sufferings of the parents still imprinted themselves on the young ones.

We even have a season totally devoted to hand-wringing, even though our culture also contains much joy, reverence, and a shared sense of community. There is a three-week period during mid-summer, devoted to lamenting our sad history. The period of lamentations begins on the seventeenth of Tammuz (*Shiva-Asar b'Tammuz*) and ends on the ninth of Av (*Tisha b'Av*), both fast days.

Observant Jews honor the mourning period by not having weddings or other joyous occasions, not cutting their hair, and not buying new clothes. The last nine days of that period see intensified mourning, during which they don't eat meat or listen to music. On the ninth of Av, the low point of the period, they also don't bathe or anoint themselves, don't wear leather shoes, and don't engage in sexual relations. They don't even study Torah, which to them must appear too joyful. Instead they read the Book of Lamentations, followed by more lamentations called *Kinnot* and/or the Book of Job.

Tisha b'Av, the end date and high point of the period of lamentation is linked to multiple calamities in our history, including the loss of our holiest worship space. The First Temple in Jerusalem was destroyed by the Babylonians in the Hebrew year 3339 (586 BCE), and the Second Temple, rebuilt after the Babylonian exile, was destroyed by the Romans in 3829 (70 CE). Somehow, the loss of the Temples is linked to irreverent or immoral behavior on the part of the Jews of that time, for which we now have to atone.

Not only Christian onlookers, but also non-orthodox American Jews like me, wonder why we should continue with this beating of one's breast and going hungry. The *Jewish Times of Baltimore* highlighted some answers in their issue of July 20, 2007.

The first response came from Rabbi Steven Schwartz of Beth El Congregation, which is quite left-wing Reform in its orientation. He said, "By fasting . . . you are expressing unity with your community, [and] . . . the fasting experience opens up the possibility of a more spiritual connection and exercise."

Hillel Zeitlin, a Jewish psychotherapist and a leader in the Orthodox community of Baltimore, expanded on that thought. He told the *Times* reporter, "Our minds relate to the world as [a physical] appetite. When we stop the constant reaching outside of ourselves, it creates a sense of calm and a truer sense of what our real needs are. Fasting is a good way to sort out one's true appetite from his false one. I think that fasting can teach us how to live differently with less."

My friend and teacher, Rabbi Geoffrey Basik, summarized all this in his 2009 pastoral letter on Tisha b'Av:

What growth and development would there be without challenges, troubles, hardships, struggles and failures? What joy would there be in "return" if we never left? How would we appreciate the good if we never experienced its absence? Reality is a dynamic between wholeness and brokenness. Living fully means embracing, and balancing, both. The High Holy Days, which are all about "return/teshuvah," are framed by tears and joy, and by two different "houses." The season begins with the destruction of one house (the Jerusalem Temple), and ends with the construction of another, the booth/sukkah, built in "the time of our joy." The entire trajectory is from Tisha B'Av to Sukkot—from grief to joy, death to rebirth, estrangement to reconciliation.

I can appreciate these "tributes to our time of weeping," but in the final analysis, I stay with my decision to pass up this ritual. Mourning the loss of old temples doesn't motive me to mourn for an entire three weeks. I find sufficient pain in remembering the Holocaust and what the Nazis did to me, my family, and my people. That pain doesn't last a day or three weeks; it's with me all the time.

I don't wish this pain away. Denying it has had terrible consequences for me in the past. For the first thirty years after I escaped from the Holocaust, I didn't speak about my experiences, nor did I ever independently bring them to mind. When asked, I said dismissively, "That was then. Now is now. I live in the present."

All that time, I lived mechanically. I ate, slept, and worked. That was all. The rest of my energy went into keeping my pain locked inside a black box within my heart.

In the end, the pain had to burst out. Luckily I was in a good location for it to happen: at a conference with a group of Lutheran ministers. I was blessed that these people could respond with sensitivity and empathy. They listened to me while I shed the tears that I had choked down.

Christian arms held me, and Christian love supported me. We Jews need to grieve, and we need Christians to give us space and understanding when we go about expressing it. So I ask my Christian readers, if you note a look of sadness in Jewish eyes, please stop blaming the victim. Instead, please remember how much it helped me to have a group of Lutheran ministers feel my pain and respect it.

Some Auschwitz survivors today project joy and gladness, but others have not been able to shake off their nightmares. Understand that, and your heart will be all the more open to my Vision of Love.

Trying Out Jerusalem

To the extent that America is a Judeo-Christian nation, the Christian part outside of my skin still overwhelms the "Judeo" part that I feel inside me.

Even New York isn't Jewish enough for some Jews, who leave town and move to Israel. I understand them. When I feel particular discomfort as an outsider in America, I find relief by going to the Land of Our Fathers.

The first time I went to Israel, in 1956, right after getting my undergraduate degree at Ohio State University, this sense of relief came as a surprise. I went there then mainly because I had majored in farm management, and this specialty seemed strange to many of my Jewish friends. When I told them about my major in college, they'd exclaim, "Oh, you must be preparing to go to Israel!" Their unspoken comment obviously was, "What kind of a career is farming for a nice Jewish boy in America?"

After the umpteenth time that I heard that reaction, I decided to see for myself what Israel offers a nice Jewish boy who wants to farm. The Ratner Foundation in Cleveland gave me a scholarship for a six-month work-study program in Israel, and soon I set sail on an Israeli ship, the *Zion,* out of New York harbor.

As soon as I got my bearings in Israel, I felt as if I had been cut loose from an invisible ball and chain. No longer did I have to watch what I said or be careful of where I trod for fear of offending Christians. The very air smelled Jewish, and I breathed it in with relief. I felt a marvelous sense of freedom, and my whole being filled with a heady sense of truly belonging to the place where I stood.

I felt a lot like Helen Schary Motro, an American-born writer and attorney, when she first traveled to Israel at age 10. She arrived as a tourist in 1959, three years after I first came there. In a Hadassah Magazine article (dated May/June 2018) she said:

> I cannot truly recall the reality of Israel from my childhood, other than the riot of color and mystery, at once austere and exotic. I didn't fall in love with the place until later. But a spark had been lit.
>
> My strong impressions eventually bloomed into *aliyah* (immigration). I returned time and time again until [in 1985], I settled down for good with my family, until it became as natural as if I had been there from the very beginning.

When my work-study program ended, I also seriously considered looking for a permanent job in Israel. I was interrupted by a letter from my draft board in the United States, informing me that if I didn't return instantly, I would face prosecution as a draft dodger. I wasn't prepared to cut all ties with America. So I went back home.

Increasingly strong family and work commitments kept me in America, but I have made many visits to Israel. Every time I land at Ben Gurion Airport, I re-experience that heady feeling, that sense of liberation, from the pressure of Christianity that envelops me in America.

That heady feeling touches on a paradox, for the Land of Israel that vivifies the Jewish spirit is also the very soil on which Jesus walked. The Land of Israel is the Holy Land that we both revere, but the followers of Jesus sheared Christianity from the Jewish mainstream. Could now be the time that this land can help launch our reconciliation?

On my third trip to Israel, I deliberately explored that question. The calendar cooperated. It was 1996, and Holy Week and Passover Week happened to practically coincide. I saw pilgrims walking the Stations of the Cross on the Via Delorosa in Jerusalem, and I watched fascinated as a man carried a huge, heavy wooden cross along the path of deliverance. I also saw Orthodox Jews walk to *shul* in their special garb, and I saw Arabs in special buses going to the Dome of the Rock for prayers.

I visited Christian sanctuaries and I peeked into back alleys with little *shtibele,* small Chasidic synagogues. I sat in services at the largest synagogue in town, a staid Episcopal church, and a German Catholic basilica.

All these places preached peace inside, but unfortunately, there was little peaceful activity outside. What I saw in the street were soldiers manning roadblocks and police on patrol with M-16 rifles. I saw a giant sign displayed in the main square in Bethlehem falsely declaring that the Jews kept pilgrims from praying at Islamic holy sites. However, I saw no street signs with directions to achieve peace!

I took my frustration to the Western Wall, the relic of the ancient Jewish Temple in Jerusalem, where pilgrims write notes to God. When I reached into my pockets to write my own note, the only thing I could find was an old bus ticket. So I wrote my note to God on the back of that ticket, pleading for the peace so lacking in the City of Peace.

Instead of peacefulness, I felt tension during my whole trip to Jerusalem. My sense of unease began the moment I made reservations for my journey. I wasn't the only pilgrim who wanted to go to Jerusalem during the spring holiday season. Travel agents in Baltimore just barely found me an available airline seat, but they were stymied in finding me a hotel room anywhere in Jerusalem.

Finally, an agent in Canada was able to squeeze me into the Seven Arches Hotel, located atop the Mount of Olives overlooking the Old City. He mentioned that this beautiful location is now an Arab neighborhood, but he assured me that it was a safe.

I didn't feel so reassured, and my feeling of unease was accentuated once I arrived at Ben Gurion International Airport. It was well after one o'clock in the morning, because planes from America arrive late, probably to accommodate connecting flights. I stepped outside and found the airport's surroundings dark and dreary.

I looked around for transportation to Jerusalem, and I was able to hail a *Sherut*. A *Sherut* is a group taxi, and before taking off, the driver arranged drop-off points for his passengers. To my dismay, he agreed to take all riders to their hotels, except for me. He proposed dropping me off at another taxi stand once we got to Jerusalem.

I didn't relish the prospect of standing alone in the dark at a taxi stand, so naturally, I protested. The taxi driver was Jewish and unshakeable. In no way was he going to drive into an Arab neighborhood.

That got me more anxious. I started asking questions. Was I in danger by getting a hotel in this neighborhood?

"No," the driver insisted.

I asked a fellow passenger who spoke better Hebrew to make sure I heard right. Yes, he agreed, the concern wasn't about safety. I soon understood that I had stumbled into some kind of turf war. Only Arab drivers served the Seven Arches Hotel. Period.

I said, "Okay, if that's the situation, please telephone for an Arab taxi to meet me at the transfer point." That didn't work either. The drop-off point for our *Sherut* was not a proper pickup point for Arab taxis—a real catch-22.

So I got out of the *Sherut* at a well-lit hotel in Jewish Jerusalem, and I found a Jewish taxi driver who reluctantly agreed to take me— at triple fare, payable in advance. The cabby roared away as soon as my feet and luggage hit the pavement outside the Seven Arches. I had to grope my way alone into the darkened building.

That scene of tension in 1996 continued, and it was oh so different from what I had experienced during my previous visit to Jerusalem in 1967. At that earlier time, shortly after the reunification of Jerusalem, people had been dancing in the streets to celebrate.

The opposite seemed to be the case now: A Jerusalem redivided. On one of my first days in town, I took a walk from my hotel. I hate walking in traffic, so I took a dusty trail that branched off from the main thoroughfare. Imagine my surprise when I rounded a bend in the trail, and it turned into a newly paved, tree-lined avenue. A light went on in my head: I had just crossed some kind of neighborhood border between Arab and Jewish Jerusalem.

Other reminders of strife kept imposing themselves upon my awareness. When I wanted to go downtown, I took Arab transportation. As I had found out upon arrival, no Jewish drivers would come to my hotel, so at first I took Arab cabs. Then I discovered a local bus that turned out to be less expensive. I found my fellow bus riders pleasant, even congenial. When I didn't have the exact fare, one of them surprised me by helping pay for my ride.

That positive touch turned back into tension when an Israeli patrol stopped the bus. Soldiers dressed in fatigues stomped into the aisle, gruffly demanding identification. My passport did it for me, but three old Arab men on the bus didn't fare as well. Soldiers seized them by the collar, pushed them off the bus, and slammed them against a wall.

The bus went on, but seeing seniors treated so gruffly stuck in my craw. When I got back to the hotel, I asked the fellow who cleaned my wing what could have caused the trouble. For his answer, he hailed a fellow employee. "Hey, Yossuf," he yelled, "show Mr. Heppner your pass!"

Yossuf showed it to me.

"Just look at it," my informant said. "It's a green pass. That takes Yossuf wherever he wants to go in Jerusalem. Now look at my pass. It is red. It means I am a prisoner of this neighborhood. I've got a college degree, but the only job I can get with this red pass is cleaning this hotel. Jewish Jerusalem is off-limits for me. Probably the guys they took off the bus only had a red pass, like me."

Before taking this trip, I had never thought I'd want to make friends with Palestinians. During my stay in Arab Jerusalem, I befriended Arabs in my hotel who clearly loved Jerusalem just as much as I do. Just to remain there, they put up with indignities that no American would tolerate. Jerusalem is our town, their town—everybody's town. It is a beautiful place that we all could share.

The Problem with Stereotypes

As you follow my exploration of a Vision of Love, you surely have noticed that I don't see myself as a "typical Jew." So if my image can't give you a clear picture of what a Jew looks like, how would you describe a "typical Jew"?

You can't trust a demeaning cartoon picturing an old Jew with a crooked nose, dirty beard, a big belly, and oversized lips. Neither can you trust the romantic picture of a young Israeli farmer with bulging biceps, wearing khaki shorts and a beanie on his head swinging a heavy hoe to weed the crops.

In truth, there is no depiction that typifies the average Jew. The Nazis, who were fanatically preoccupied with the appearance of "racially pure" people, once selected a blonde German girl as the epitome of Aryan. They were horrified to discover that the girl they had selected for their "Aryan" poster actually was Jewish. They must have turned purple as they tore down the billboards with her picture on it.

During my first stay in Israel, I roomed with a Jewish immigrant from India who looked like many people's image of a typical Hindu.

I have a new friend in Israel who comes from Ethiopia and looks like a Coptic black prince. I have friends in the United States who are black and call themselves Jewish, and I'm not just talking about converts. I could go on, but I think you got my point that there is no standard way to characterize a Jew, just like there's no "standard" for picturing a Catholic.

That said, I often recognize a stranger as Jewish even before we are introduced. That is easier to do in America than, say, in Israel, because most American Jews descend from Eastern European immigrants. People in this demographic branch of Jews are called Ashkenazim, derived from the Hebrew word *Ashkenaz,* meaning German. Most Ashkenazim, like me, for example, have German names even if we are born in other countries, located generally to the east of Germany. The Ashkenazim have their own language, called Yiddish, which is derived from early German.

Members of the other main demographic branch are called Sephardim, derived from the Hebrew word *Sepharad,* meaning Spain. Most Sephardim have Spanish names even though they may be from families living anywhere around the Mediterranean. The Sephardim also have their own language, called Ladino, which is derived from early Spanish.

For example, the first Jewish Supreme Court justice, Louis Brandeis, was Ashkenazi and has a German name (meaning "branding iron"), even though his family came to the United States from Czechoslovakia. By contrast, the second Jewish Supreme Court justice, Benjamin Cardozo, was Sephardi and has a Spanish name (meaning "goldfinch" in Aragonese, a Spanish dialect), even though his family came from Portugal.

The first wave of Jewish immigrants to America was Sephardic, but the majority of Jews who came later was Ashkenazic. We Ashkenazi Jews have a recognizably common range of appearance and demeanor, and so, in fact, do many Sephardi Jews. That makes it easier for us to identify each other.

Furthermore, consciously or unconsciously, when I meet new people, I also send out certain clues and nuances to proclaim my background and vice versa. Give me a roomful of my neighbors, and I can quickly classify them in categories like "almost certainly Jewish," or "likely Jewish," or "likely non-Jewish," or "almost certainly non-Jewish." I will lay a ten-to-one bet that I'm 90 percent accurate.

The hedge in my bet indicates that I can't be sure I'm accurate, because my clues aren't totally reliable. This situation leads to film and TV productions that strike the funny bone precisely because we are surprised if we make a mistake. You may remember the Amish character who lends humor to the movie *The Frisco Kid,* and you ought to see the lesser-known but hilarious French production *If I Lie,* depicting an Armenian who passes himself off as Jewish to escape his persecutors.

It's easier to form a mental image of a Jewish person than, let's say, a Catholic, because Jews are a people as well as a religion. This distinction still can be hard to nail down exactly. The government of the new State of Israel found that out when they passed their unique Law of Return. It promised immediate citizenship to any Jew who applied. However, they soon ran into trouble for lack of a clear definition of "Who is a Jew."

This issue became acute when many "Jews" asked for admission after the collapse of the Soviet Union. Many applicants turned out to be people who had never entered a synagogue and who ate ham and cheese sandwiches at Yom Kippur.

This challenge became even more acute when another group of would-be Jews, the so-called Falash Murah from Ethiopia, applied for entry under the "Law of Return," even though their Jewish ancestry is questionable.

So, yes, no one can tell for sure whether a certain person is Jewish or not. Looking for "Jewish" characteristics can easily lead to stereotyping, which I absolutely hate.

Therefore, it came as a big surprise to me when my friend Joy unexpectedly accused me of stereotyping her very own self. The accusation came in the middle of a conversation when, innocently, I took a "linguistic shortcut" to explain a difference in our viewpoints. I called her "Quintessentially Christian."

Immediately she challenged me. "What do you mean by that?"

I tried to explain it calmly: "I mean that you dress like a Christian, think like a Christian, speak like a Christian, and look at life from a Christian point of view!"

This didn't work at all. "Oh," she said. "Is it something like calling out a Jew because he looks too Jewish?"

I was dumbfounded and didn't respond right away. She lunged into the breach.

"You make me feel less than," Joy said heatedly. "Do you see something wrong about my way of dressing, my way of speaking, my way of thinking? I feel labeled as if you slapped my forehead with a stamp that says, *Damaged goods. Product Rejected.*"

Try as I might, I couldn't find words that say, without offense, that Jews can pick out a typical Christian from a crowd. Not all Christians, just those deeply into a Christian way of dealing with life.

I said, "If I recognize typical Christian behavior, that doesn't mean I criticize it, demean it, or harbor suspicions about it. I am nonplussed at seeing that the tables are turned when it comes to using stereotypes. I thought I was way beyond slapping labels on people."

"You went way beyond labeling," she came back. "You have ripped at my belief in Christianity, implying that there is something wrong with it."

Of course I denied ripping at anything, but it didn't help to assuage her feeling that I had slung a slur.

Getting more and more upset, she asked, "Why do I get the brunt of the Jewish issue? In a lifetime of being a practicing Christian, I have not heard anyone among my family and friends bad-mouthing Jews."

"If I describe how I see or interpret you, how can you call that "bad-mouthing?'" I said.

"That's the way it lands," she replied. "So why can't you come right out and admit you slipped into a stereotype, that you didn't just select a figure of speech."

"Forgive me," I said. "I can't explain why I used that expression any better than I have already. I'm sorry it brought you pain."

"Jews don't have a monopoly on feeling pain," Joy said. She thought a moment, and then continued more appeasingly. "I know. You have endured poor attitudes and much, much worse. Still, as a Christian, I want you to understand that, just like you, I can feel hurt when people come at me with poor expressions and slanted attitudes. Show some compassion for the rocks in my shoes."

I gave it a try. "You hate being labeled," I said, "because in a sense, a label accuses you of something without a chance to defend yourself. The label plain and simple pushes you out of the conversation."

"True," she said. "But you still haven't told me what prompted you to call me 'quintessentially Christian.' I'd also still would like to know the specific ways in which you think Christians act or respond that irritate, anger, or annoy you as a Jew."

To lighten up the conversation I said, "Come on, Joy, let me answer in a 'quintessentially Jewish' way. I'll tell you a story and in the process, maybe you'll realize that I understand you."

She still was afraid that I was sidestepping the issue, but she gave me a nod to go ahead.

I told her that when I was at Ohio State University, I dated a Catholic girl whom I liked a lot. A Jewish friend of mine didn't recognize her as one of "our crowd," so he asked me, "Who was that girl that you took to the dance last Saturday night?"

I answered, "Mary Jane Taylor."

"Oh," he said in Yiddish. *"A emmishe Yiddishe nomme."*

"Literally, that translates to 'a truly Jewish name.' Obviously, his choice of words evidenced sarcasm, but I don't think there was any rancor in it. He was just conveying his recognition that my date carried—to use that term again—a quintessentially Christian name."

Joy eventually understood I had meant no harm, and I understood that stereotyping can be inflicted in ways other than telling nasty jokes. She ended our discussion with healing words with which she knew I could agree.

"At the end of the road," she said, "we must stay aware that we touch another person's life by the way we live our own. I feel a lot of wonderment about that Jewish world of yours. I wonder if you have that same sense about my Christian world? I shudder to think you're repulsed by it. Whatever you think about it, don't close off your Jewish world from me by categorizing me as unable to grasp the essence of it."

I don't come out looking good in relating this interchange. I tell it to show that raw sensitivities come to the fore in a Jewish-Christian dialogue.

If we choose to have such a dialogue, we have to watch our words carefully even if we feel free and open with each other. We have to remain aware that what seems like a "normal" expression to the speaker can have hurtful connotations to the listener.

Our choice of words can subliminally indicate our discomfort with the dialogue. So, I'll come right out with it, although not without blushing: I, who dialogue whenever I can, day or night, even I am not completely comfortable in speaking about a sensitive issue with a Christian.

In other Jews, this discomfort can take an extreme form, and in this context an extreme event in my first marriage comes to mind.

One of my in-laws was married to a Christian woman. Well, they weren't formally married, but they had a long-term common-law union. I don't know the woman's name, and I never met her because her husband never brought her to family affairs.

More incredibly, he hid the woman from his family. The couple had a house together, and normally both of them lived there. But the man steadfastly maintained to his family that he lived elsewhere, and he actually bought an extra house to support this fiction. The house was completely furnished but was in actual use only when he invited family. His wife apparently never set foot in it.

This state of affairs was an open secret, but no one in the family had the nerve to talk about it. Perhaps we recognized in our own hearts the demons that caused him to perpetuate this crazy fiction.

I'll go further and admit that the Jewish discomfort with Christians can come to the fore in ways more demeaning than a choice of where and how to maintain one's home.

I know Jews who are scrupulously honest in business deals with other Jews but don't seem to be bothered by cheating a Christian customer. A story illustrating this point was told to me by a Jewish accountant specializing in real estate transactions:

After helping a client close the books on a complex case, my friend noticed that there still were several thousands of dollars remaining in escrow, and he checked with the client about returning the balance.

The client pulled at his black beard and seemed engrossed in thought. Then he said, "This situation reminds me of a ruling by Rabbi Eleazar of Minsk on unintentionally enriching one's self at another's expense. Do you know what his ruling was?" He answered himself with a sardonic smile: saying "Fuck 'em!"

There never was a Rabbi Eleazar of Minsk, and a true Jewish scholar would not utter such an obscenity. Nonetheless, there's no denying that the bitter taste in Jewish mouths resulting from Christian persecution has made some Jews feel justified in unleashing what they think to be a valid retaliation.

I don't cheat Christians, and I don't sling slurs. Nonetheless, the remnants of a bitter taste apparently still reside in my own mouth, and that must have registered with my friend Joy. We Jews must find an antidote to our bitterness if we wish to taste the sweetness in the Vision of Love.

Confronting "Who Killed Jesus?"

The issue of "Who killed Jesus?" has curbed cordial relations between Christians and Jews for centuries. "You damned Jews killed Jesus!" still remains the battle cry of Jew-bashers.

You can't shrug off this battle cry as the pastime of anti-Semitic nincompoops. The problem remains impactful because even fair-minded readers of the New Testament see "the Jews" depicted as the murderers of Jesus.

Marc Chagall expressed that depiction vividly in a painting called *Yellow Crucifixion.* He painted it in 1943, at the height of the Holocaust. Look it up online, and you can see firsthand the horror that this image engenders.

Nazis didn't venerate Jesus, but they used the incrimination of Jews in Scripture to incite people to hatred. The Gospels of Matthew and Luke in particular inflame readers against us. These passages describe the scene as Roman occupation forces in Palestine arrange the planned execution of two alleged wrongdoers.

One victim is Jesus Christus; the other one is Jesus Barabbas. The Gospels explain that the Romans were offering convicts a kind of amnesty in honor of some Roman festival. Sardonically, the presiding officer, Pontius Pilatus, offered the crowd to pick just one of the two condemned men to be saved. The crowd yelled to have Barabbas saved, strongly implying that Jesus was the one that the crowd wanted crucified.

Matthew 27, as translated in the NIV, depicts this scene at its worst for us Jews:

> So when Pilate saw that he could do nothing,
> but rather that a riot was beginning, he took some
> water and washed his hands before the crowd,
> saying, "I am innocent of this man's blood; see to it
> yourselves." Then the people as a whole answered,
> "His blood be on us and on our children!"

It implies to even a cursory reader that the Jews at the scene were not powerless, passive onlookers, but rather they were a crowd that enthusiastically cheered a murder and "didn't give a damn" if they would forever be blamed for it. They are pictured as happily bestowing the curse for their guilt onto every single future Jewish child.

I am a Jewish child, a child survivor of the Holocaust. I interpret that passage to mean that my Holocaust experience was my just desserts, an actualization of the curse from Matthew. Worse yet, the passage implies that even the Holocaust can't lift the curse. It seems to invite a new edition of the Holocaust to rid the world of us guilty Jewish children once and for all.

This line of thought has led to a huge problem for Jews, not because one more human being was executed but because Scripture interprets the event to mean that "the Jews" killed God. Murdering a deity is no minor matter. Those responsible literally kill the Source of Salvation!

Of course, I personally don't believe God can be killed, but others do believe so. For nearly two thousand years, a myriad of angry voices have vowed vengeance upon the Jews because of the Scriptural depiction of the death of Jesus. There's no denying that some of the most damaging voices demanding vengeance spoke from pulpits in Christian churches.

For this reason, the entire Passion of Jesus cries for a new interpretation. Few Christian schools have attempted this, but I have heard it done in the Jewish Sunday School I attended in the late 1940s.

Rabbi Enoch Kronheim, a remarkably gentle man, taught our high-school-level class in Cleveland, Ohio, and I remember his interpretation of "who killed Jesus" as if I heard it yesterday.

His approach would have been amazing for any Jewish teacher of that day, but it was uniquely amazing for him and our class. Rabbi Kronheim himself was a refugee from Nazi Germany, and every single one of us students had experienced personal losses due to the Nazi murder campaign in Europe lending a huge significance to Rabbi Kronheim's interpretation.

Our rabbi taught that the New Testament is a valued and influential work, but that the Gospel writers were not historians. They wrote their accounts from the viewpoint of thirty to fifty years after the death of Christ. They were addressing a very specific audience, all victims of the Romans, whose terror tactics to suppress rebellion had become even more extreme than at the time of Jesus.

If the nascent Christian Church wanted to survive, their stance toward the Roman oppressors needed to be as appeasing as possible. The Gospel version of the Passion of Jesus was intentionally slanted to make them minimally objectionable to Romans; the only ones standing to take the blame for the Crucifixion were "the Jews."

When the Gospel writes were crafting their stories, traditional Jews rejected the elevation of Jesus to become the Messiah. Therefore, the Gospel writers directed their efforts to spread their Gospel to pagans, who reveled in fantastic tales about the life and death of various gods. The Gospels cleverly employed the same dramatic language and religious symbology that pagans already knew about the life and death of the various gods on Mt. Olympus. The Gospel stories passed down over the century aren't history; they are homily.

Even though I was only a young teenager when I studied with Rabbi Kronheim, his take on the Passion of Christ has helped me feel, deep in my heart, the personal agony Christians feel over losing the Living Christ on Earth. Rabbi Kronheim emphasized that instead of a narrative intended to damn Jews, the Gospels were crafted to convince people that the crucified Jesus ties Christians to a life with God that is vivid, vital, and uplifting.

However, even if you understand that the crucifixion took on the centrality of Christian dogma—the "Gospel Truth," this doesn't take away from the fact that it has caused major problems for us Jews. There is extreme danger in dramatizing what Peter said, not because he said it to the Corinthians but because his words are taken literally by modern-day listeners. Jews come out looking as if we denigrate the central event of Christian theology.

Gospel writers probably considered themselves prophets, and they should be understood on the level of the grand exhortations of prophets like Isaiah and Jeremiah. I place their story of the Passion of Christ on a level with the account of the Revelation of the Torah at Mount Sinai.

I love the vivid Biblical depiction of the "Giving of the Law" amid thunder claps and lighting flashes. Set beside the Revelation at Sinai, the Passion comes out just as vivid.

Neither the Passion of Christ nor the Giving of the Law, however, is a historical account about events occurring in the Middle East thousands of years ago. Historicity really doesn't matter. The importance lies in our response to the story.

When I regard Moses descending the mountain, tablets of the law in hand, I see a lesson about a caring God; when a Christian regards the passion of Jesus on the cross, he can see the importance of man's relationship to other men and to God.

The words in these passages were intended to make a moral point. They use vivid imagery, and readers understand the imagery at gut level. Even today, people find the Passion of Christ amazingly gripping, as is evident from the popular Mel Gibson movie released in 2006 that graphically depicts this scene. We must get hold of ourselves, lest the gut response to the imagery keeps undermining progress toward my Vision of Love.

11.
Implementing the Vision

While the Christian Testament has multiple accounts of the Passion of Jesus, the Torah has only one version that describes Moses' descent of Mount Sinai with his two tablets, even though he brings them down twice.

Furthermore, there is no corroborating information about the entire Exodus episode in any other chronicle, even though it figures so centrally in Jewish lore. Ancient Egyptian history, otherwise amazingly well preserved, makes no mention that any Hebrews ever lived there, not even Moses, although Exodus relates that he was adopted into Egyptian royalty.

By comparison, the information about the life and times of Jesus is voluminous. We can't pinpoint the true location of Mount Sinai in the Moses story, but we know precisely where to find Bethlehem and Nazareth, where Jesus walked. The wealth of corroborating and ancillary information about the time of Jesus makes it possible to put a new spin on the Passion of Jesus.

Putting Compassion into the Passion

I envision four ways to see the Passion with more dispassionate eyes. Any new view of this type, if taught in Christian churches and Sunday schools, would transform the crucifixion story by adding "com" to "passion," in order to take the onus of the *Passio* off the backs of us Jews.

No doubt, attempting a new slant on Scripture venerated for two millennia is a touchy venture. Yet we have to undertake it if we want to implement my Vision of Love. Therefore, I suggest that the Crucifixion passages in Scripture be read in a new light, and that shines on four aspects:

• **The parable** in the story;

• **The politics** at the time of the story;

• **The cast of characters** involved in the story; and/or

• **The theological intent** of the story.

The parable in the story can be best understood by rereading the scene in Matthew 27 just before the crucifixion, when the presiding officer, Pontius Pilatus, shows a mass of people two accused prisoners.

> Now it was the governor's custom at the festival
> to release a prisoner chosen by the crowd.
> At that time they had a well-known prisoner
> whose name was Jesus Barabbas.
> So when the crowd had gathered, Pilate asked them,
> "Which one do you want me to release to you:
> Jesus Barabbas, or Jesus who is called the Messiah?"

In Hebrew, the second prisoner's name is Jesus Bar-Abba, which translates to "Jesus, Son of the Father." The Hebrew clarifies the parable: When you put Bar-Abba next to Christus, the crowd saves the Son of the Father in preference over the (not-yet-proclaimed) Messiah. Even if Jesus were already seen as a Christus (Messiah) at the crucifixion, he would be seen as "just" a human being, not as a "Bar-Abba," a real Son of God. If the story in the Gospels had been slanted to Jewish belief, the choice of "the Jewish crowd" would be more understandable. Instead, the parable is slanted to discredit this "Jewish" image of Jesus.

I imagine that later Church fathers wanted to suppress the original version of the two convicts about to be executed, so that the whole comparison was made to disappear from the Gospels. If the original version had been left standing, it would admit that there could be an alternate view to Jesus' stature as Son of God. The parable then changed into a justification for damning the Jews who didn't follow the early Christians on their new religious path.

Seen in this light, the Jesus versus Barabbas segment in the Passion of Christ would not make Jews responsible for the crucifixion of Jesus, but would instead be about makings sure that the prisoner they chose to save was the one entitled to be called the Son of God. Thus the discussion would be about politics, not about a judgment of guilt.

The politics at the time of the story require us to view the Crucifixion as an act of policy on the part of those dominant and threatening Romans who ruled over Judea at the time of the historical Jesus and the early Church. These occupiers didn't allow anything to happen that could possibly undermine their power and domination. Therefore, a trial for Jesus would not have taken place if it hadn't been in the political interest of the Romans.

In the lifetime of Jesus, the people of Judah lived in chaos and despair. King Herod Antipas ruled with an iron hand as a vassal of the Romans, and the Jewish religious-political infrastructure was crumbling. Moral values were in decline. It was a hopeless time, ripe for the arrival of a Messiah.

Jesus was not the only candidate for the position. Other charismatic figures arose at the time and were embraced as a Messiah by some of the people living in Roman-occupied Judea. However, these other messianic claims soon proved self-serving and lacking in integrity, and Jesus greatly exceeded the success and renown of the other would-be messiahs.

As long as would-be messiahs followed a purely religious path, they probably didn't greatly disturb the Roman occupiers. The Romans were concerned much more interested in muzzling rabble-rousers, of which there also were many. In fact, during the time Jesus preached, at least two actual insurrections took place. The Romans quickly and successfully crushed these uprisings and punished the whole nation with reprisals. Alarm at yet another possible insurrection motivated the arrest of Jesus.

The preaching of Jesus raised an alarm because he taught that the Kingdom of God had arrived, and some people started calling him "the King of the Jews." Jesus clarified that he was talking about a spiritual kingdom, but still a number of his remarks indicate that he deplored the political situation. He even seems to have favored armed struggle to get rid of the Romans. So it's not surprising that the Romans cast a suspicious eye on him, not so much as a religious figure but as a real or actual political threat.

Crucifixion however, was a widespread Roman terror tactic. Dr. Leonard Shlain, an ethical philosopher in Mill Valley, California told me that in 4 BC, the Romans arrested two thousand Jews in Galilee for sedition, crucified them and left their rotting corpses on a forest of crosses as a warning to others. Jesus Christ, Dr. Shlain pointed out, was only one of many unfortunates who were punished by the Romans in this way.

The point of this analysis is that the Romans—and no one else—controlled governmental functions in Judea. If anyone was executed, the cruel Roman administration was behind it. Jesus violated no religious precept or any Jewish law. However, no Jewish court ever sentenced convicts to be crucified.

The cast of characters involved in the story would reveal "who was who" at the time of the crucifixion. During the lifetime of Jesus, the entire native population of Judea and Galilee was Jewish. All the figures involved in the story of the Passion of Christ who weren't Romans were Jews, including Jesus himself.

No one alive at the time of Christ thought of him or herself as a Christian because the term and the concept had not yet been invented. All Jews, including Jesus, felt the heavy hand of Roman oppression equally. From that viewpoint, the prosecution of Jesus can't be a case of "us against them." All of "us" were Jews. We were all equally oppressed.

The theological intent of the Passion of Christ covers the mystery behind the events described in Scripture. It is far more important to understand why the death of Jesus had to happen rather than to struggle with who made it happen.

The New Testament clearly indicates that God intended the Crucifixion to happen. The "mystery" of the death of Jesus says he accepted death to alleviate the burden of sin. As a Jew, I lack a personage who can shoulder sin for me, but I understand the concept. It underlies the spiritual work we do on the Day of Atonement, our Yom Kippur.

The crystal clear messages I read in the gospels is that theologically, Jesus Christ had to die for Salvation to happen.

In addition to these four clarifications, there must be others. I want any new positive interpretation to be actualized, whether it is my light on the matter or that of others. I plead for Church leaders to select, promulgate, and spread such interpretations, so that in the future, Church teachings on the crucifixion of Jesus won't motivate another outraged Christian to storm out of a sermon to beat up on a Jew.

In *Nostra Aetate,* a Vatican encyclical promulgated on October 28, 1965, Pope Paul VI took a big step in that direction. I heartily applaud this promulgation, which appears in detail in Appendix A of this book. A key portions says:

> What happened in His passion cannot be charged against all the Jews, without distinction, then alive, nor against the Jews of today. Although the Church is the new people of God, the

Jews should not be presented as rejected or accursed by God, as if this followed from the Holy Scriptures.

All should see to it, then, that in catechetical work or in the preaching of the word of God, they do not teach anything that does not conform to the truth of the Gospel and the spirit of Christ."

As policy, the encyclical is an excellent first step. However, I think specific actions and practices need to be instituted so that religious services "do not teach anything that does not conform" to the new way of dealing with the Jews.

Unfortunately, the notion of Jews as the enemy of the Church pervades Church teachings, making revision difficult. The very decorations of the beautiful medieval churches for which Europe is famous encourage scapegoating of Jews.

To get a visceral sense of that, go to the Cathedral of Erfurt, Germany, as suggested by my teacher Rabbi David Zaslow. A damning message of mistrust and hate is carved on the very benches on which choir of the Erfurt Cathedral still sits today.

The carving depicts *Ecclesia,* the spirit of the Church, sitting on a fine horse, carrying the Christian symbol of the fish in one hand. With a lance in her other hand, she attacks *Synagoga,* the spirit of the Synagogue, in a joust intended to knock *Synagoga* off her own steed—a pig! (Rabbi Zaslow's research is detailed in his work: *Roots and Branches: A Sourcebook for Understanding the Jewish Roots of Christianity, Replacement Theology, and Anti-Semitism* [Perfect Paperback, 2011].)

Amos Elon's book, *The Pity of It All,* which I cited earlier, underscores the same point. In his comprehensive historical portrait of Jews in Germany, Elon explains:

The notorious *Judensau* (Jews' sow) was a common subject of Christian religious art and propaganda. Bas-reliefs and cartoons of the *Judensau*—always shown with bearded rabbis who suck and lick its excrement . . . were displayed in the great cathedrals [of Germany and even] outside the *Schloskirche* in Wittenberg (where Luther posted his ninety-five theses). . .

A famous *Judensau* was displayed on the main bridge leading into the city of Frankfurt, affixed there not by some bigoted individual but by the city government.

Pre-modern worshipers were acutely aware of the scenes depicted in their churches and around their towns. They understood Jews depicted as pigs and other demeaning symbols better than Scripture, which they weren't allowed to read even if they were literate (which most of them were not).

It is no coincidence that the Nazis who dragged my mother off to prison in 1942 called her a *sau*. (Germans spell the word "sow" differently, but they pronounce it the same as in English.) I heard it with my own ears, some five hundred years after the benches at Erfurt were carved and the bridge at Frankfurt was decorated.

Except for adornments with Jews as pigs and donkeys, medieval European cathedrals are beautiful structures. That presents a challenge: If today's stewards of these architectural treasures would want to get rid of these defacements, how would they go about it? Probably, they shouldn't try. Instead, it might help to place a plaque beneath each depiction deploring the misconceptions of yore and affirming today's brotherhood between *Ecclesia* and *Synagoga*.

As for the Church in general, I think it should not only support a plaque for Erfurt and other Church centers but also publicly abrogate the offending sources in Scripture each time they are presented from the pulpit.

When I suggest not only plaques for benches, but also abrogating Scripture, many are aghast. They say, "What kind of Pandora's box are you proposing to open? If you can change Scripture to suit your needs, can't anybody change Scripture to suit themselves? Do you want thieves to alter the Ten Commandments so that they can steal with impunity?"

I answer, "No, but the very existence of a New Testament shows that changes in Scripture have been necessary in the past. Changes were written into religious law and promptly implemented because new realities demanded such changes."

Even the Torah itself has turned earlier dictums on their head. For example, take the legal principle, understood throughout Scripture, that a family's real estate holdings should pass as an inheritance to the eldest son in each generation. Torah sets out a specific ruling for a case when an eldest son dies childless.

Called the Levirate Law (Deuteronomy 25:5–10), it requires the next-eldest son in the family to marry his elder brother's widow, so that the marriage can provide the family with a surrogate "first son" as heir to the real estate. In case no brother is available, the responsibility falls on the nearest male relative.

Earlier Scripture (Genesis 38) illustrates how the Levirate Law was being implemented. In the story, Er, the son of the patriarch Judah, marries a woman named Tamar. Er dies young, unable to sire a son to inherit the family's land. Two younger brothers in succession also try and fail at the task. Eventually, Judah himself takes it on and succeeds, leading to a positive ending.

The entire Book of Ruth also has Levirate Law as its leitmotiv. In this case, no brothers-in-law are available to recently widowed Ruth, and the levirate requirement falls on her late husband's cousins.

The first cousin she approaches declines, but another cousin, the highly respected Boaz, carries out the law. In the process he falls deeply in love with Ruth, thereby giving the Book of Ruth another wonderfully positive ending.

The Levirate Law described with such detail early in Torah and again in the Book of Ruth is overruled in Leviticus 18:16, which obviously was written at a later date. It outright forbids a man to marry his sister-in-law, because of the then-negative view on polyg-amy and/or intermarriage among close relations.

The Levirate Law itself has a "way out," an escape clause from its provisions, called *Chalitzah,* that the male in-law of a widow can invoke to refuse marrying her (see Deuteronomy 25:9–10), and this was used by one of Ruth's in-laws, as I mentioned above.

That escape clause is now the operative rule, meaning that an in-law impacted by this law is now *required* to always invoke the *Chalitzah* clause, and the refused widow has to respond in a stylized, cultic ceremony. She must spit in the in-law's face and take off one of his shoes, so that all of his relatives and acquaintances can label him "shoeless weakling." These details seem comical, but Ortho-dox Jews still practice *Chalitzah* as an obligatory, open disavowal of Torah law.

An even more central Biblical commandment, one prohibiting false swearing (Leviticus 19:12), also has been abrogated in Jewish practice. It is famous as one of the Big Ten Commandments, so to have it nullified may seem surprising. The relevant ceremony comes dramatically at the start of Yom Kippur, the Day of Atonement, the absolute holiest day in the Jewish religious calendar.

The abrogation ceremony, called *Kol Nidre,* recalls a tragic era, the time of the Catholic Inquisition. The wording gives Jews per-mission to swear falsely when confronted by the "inquisitors" of the Roman Catholic Inquisition and similar persecutors. Swearing to tell the truth and doing so with inquisitors and persecutors could easily cost a person his Jewish head.

I use these precedents to propose taking the sting out of the "who killed Jesus" issue. Church authorities could devise a ceremony similar to *Kol Nidre,* declaring that Jews of today bear absolutely no guilt for the death of Jesus. The abrogation would be mandatory at every celebration of the Passion. To use the words of the late Pope Benedict XVI, it would publicly ask congregants to see Jews as fully respected brothers and sisters before God.

A Catholic priest from Los Angeles actually tried to institute such a proclamation, but he couldn't make it work. He explained his plight graphically. (See "A Legacy of Blood: Can Christianity Be Purged of Anti-Semitism Without Changing the Gospels?" by Ben Birnbaum, *Moment Magazine,* October 2001, page 50 ff.). He said:

> I may understand the context, but the parishioners don't. I can't give them context along with everything else I'm supposed to teach them in the seven minutes I'm allowed for my homily.

I hope other priests successfully stop the calumny of deicide in the Easter service. If it requires hard work, that doesn't make it impossible. An annual, public declaration from the pulpit is essential if we are to overcome the pain and separation generated by the issue of "who killed Jesus." It is an absolute prerequisite to activating my Vision of Love.

Jewish and Christian Views of Love

Some Christians, with a disdainful look at Judaism, like to say, "Yours is a religion of law, while ours is a religion of love."

This characterization is far from true because love occupies a central position in Jewish life and Jewish services. Judaism has a basic tenet, proclaiming *Olam Chesed Yivneh,* which means (approximately), "The World is structured on God's Love." This tenet is virtually the same as "God's Love is sent to earth as Jesus," or at least the two concepts are compatible.

Key Jewish prayers also have love as their theme: Love of God for mankind (in the *Ahava Rabba* prayer), mankind's love for God (in the *Vahavta* Prayer), and mankind's love for one another (in the *Alenu* Prayer). They all are found in the standard Jewish prayer books.

Jewish sages emphasize love, just like Jesus, and Jesus, in preaching about love, uses totally Jewish expressions. Jesus appears to have been a follower of Rabbi Hillel the Elder, the acknowledged religious leader of the previous generation, and both spoke about loving one's neighbor with the same emphasis and almost the same terms.

When Hillel was challenged to sum up Jewish lore "while standing on one foot," he said, "What is hateful to you, do not do to your neighbor" (Talmud, Shabbat 31a). When similarly challenged to name "the great commandment in the Law," Jesus responded that it is to love God and to "love your neighbor as yourself. On these two commandments depend all the law and the prophets" (Matthew 22:35–40). Both clearly based their response on the original Biblical precept of "love your neighbor as yourself" (Leviticus 19:18).

I can't deny, however, that Gospel writers do talk about love a whole lot more than the Talmudic sages. Holly Golightly and the Apostle John can sound remarkably alike. John can come across as truly effusive (NIV, 1 John 4): "Dear Friends, let us love one another, for love comes from God. Everyone who loves has been born of God and knows God."

The Talmud doesn't talk like that. As my friend Fred Katz rightly says, "Judaism is more inherently focused on justice than loving outreach."

When I take a closer look, however, I don't see such a huge difference between the two religions on the subject of love. Promoting "Justice, justice shalt thou pursue," (Deuteronomy 16:18–20) brings about a loving, brotherly society at least as much as promulgating, "Dear Friends, let us love one another."

Maybe it's worth digging into a very legalistic sounding passage in the Talmud to pin down that it promotes love in a practical way. If we understand this one example, then the Judaic outlook may not sound so different.

The passage I've chosen, Bava Metzia 58B, first posits that

enmity is the opposite of love. Enmity originates, the sages say, when you see "your neighbor" as odd or weird. Considering him weird quickly descends to calling him names, slandering his character, and passing along rumors that criticize his behavior. Demonic descriptions and nasty gossip dehumanize "your neighbor" so quickly that it soon becomes okay to treat him in ways as horrible as the names he was called. It leads to taking away his rights and eventually even his right to live.

The sages particularly focus on defaming a person's character. For example, the Tanna said, "Anyone who shames another person in public is as if he sheds his blood." And Rav Nachman bar Yitzchak said to the Tanna, "You say well. For when a person is publicly shamed, we see that the red blush of his face disappears and whiteness takes its place."

Later Jewish law delves even deeper into this issue. It forbids telling unflattering stories about your neighbor, even if the neighbor's missteps are true and verifiable. Telling stories about him still casts aspersions on his character, and loving your neighbor means that you carefully guard his reputation. If you have a problem with him, you deal with him directly; you don't get back at him by taking your dissatisfaction to other neighbors. Even if you don't resolve your issue with a problem neighbor, you are honor bound to shut up about it.

Another Talmudic discussion raises "loving your neighbor" to the level of self-talk. The sages said, "When you judge your neighbor, extend to him an extra measure of merit." That means when you "weigh" your thoughts about your neighbor, balance the negative with extra positive thoughts so that the pendulum swings in his favor.

Up until today, leading rabbis have given well-attended lectures warning against defaming your neighbor. "Keeping a pure tongue" is a feature of study groups aimed at bringing this aspect of "love" into regular daily practice.

Even secular Jews pursue this theme, as for example in an e-mail recently posted by one of my online friends. He wrote:

> It is with great insight that our elders teach us that the sin of defamation exceeds that of murder. When one murders another, there are only two people involved, perpetrator and victim. But when you slander, everyone who has heard the slander becomes a victim, along with the perpetrator and victim. Our relationship to our Source has always been as an integral community, not solely as individuals. It is as an integral community that we survive.

Even if Judaism and Christianity both provide ample encouragement to be loving, sadly, love does not prevail in our world, not even in Israel, the land trod by both Rabbi Hillel of the Jews and Rabbi Jesus of the Christians. I don't even find my own self reaching out with total love toward Palestinians. However, when I pause to reflect, I realize that hate comes out of fear. Jews and Palestinians fear the same thing: Being left homeless and defenseless.

Clearly, we can find our way back to love in the Middle East if we realize the issue is not about a lack of love, but rather a lack of security. That lack is not hard to correct in reality; the feeling of security is only a frame of mind. If I say I'm secure, then I'm secure. And if I feel secure, I can send love-energy to Palestinians so they can overcome the fear that equally plagues the Israelis.

Meditating in my home in America, I imagine an Arab Palestinian counterpart, a *doppelgänger*, who looks just like me. I have given him a name, "Yussif," and I tell him I understand his pain, and I send him positive vibes of love. It's a way of applying the commandment to "Love my neighbor as myself," which is difficult for me to do in reality because where would I be able to safely meet such a neighbor?

Some Israeli Jews have in fact been able to put this "love of neighbor" into practice in relating to Israeli Arabs. In Neve Shalom

(Oasis of Peace), a village not far from Tel Aviv, Arabs and Jews live together in an intentional community founded by a Catholic priest. The binational village is unique and harbors a School of Interpersonal Relations. Arab and Jewish children and adults work together to find a common vocabulary so that they can talk to and work with one another peacefully.

When I visited Neve Shalom, I took the opportunity to meet its then-executive director, who is an Arab. He overtly acted caring toward me and toward Jews in general, even though he naturally is full of concern for the future of his own people. I belong to an organization that supports this village, and we join in its efforts to send a message of love and peace to all troubled peoples.

The tough challenge of promoting love out there in Israel doesn't differ all that much from the challenge of maintaining love right here in our own home with our own family. It's all about fear.

I experienced that myself. My late wife, Shana, was a pack rat. She couldn't bring herself to throw anything away because, who knows? Someday somebody she loves might need it. To me, the stuff she stored looked like a mess, until I came to see the mess as congealed love.

In thinking more broadly about love, it puzzles me why we don't make better use of it in getting along with other religions. Comparisons between the words of Jesus and Moses, Apostle John, and Rabbi Akiva become irrelevant when we operate in an environment of love. The Kabbalah teaches that love energy flows from God continually, like electricity down a wire. All we need to do to access it is to turn on a switch in our minds.

So, even if Jews don't often talk like Christians who say, "God is love," Jewish people still believe that love is God's biggest and most pervasive gift. Taking "loving our neighbors" as a heavenly commandment provides an excellent means to implement my Vision of Love.

A Peace Agreement Between Jews and Christians

Important as it is, an exhortation to "love your neighbor" can't be imposed by superior power. While Jewish law demands it, no authority has found a way to enforce it.

In 1995, the U.S. government tried hard to impose a peace agreement on warring faith communities in the former Yugoslavia. While they acceded to attend a peace conference in Dayton, Ohio, their issues still remain basically unresolved even today.

I was personally involved in trying to actualize a Jewish-Christian peace agreement in Columbia, Maryland, a "new town" between Washington and Baltimore. The parties involved had far more input into the agreement than those summoned to Dayton, Ohio, and they actively tried to make their agreement work.

Still, they had only limited success. It is hard to institute brotherly behavior that is both successful and enduring. Here is what I experienced:

In 1972, I moved to Columbia, which today still operates under covenants imposed by the Rouse Company, the super-developer of Columbia New Town.

One of these covenants imposed the developer's belief that people of various religions should live side by side and interact cooperatively. Rouse enforced that by forbidding congregations to build houses of worship in Columbia. To replace churches and synagogues, Rouse built so-called Interfaith Centers, and had them work out shared space and time.

At the time, I belonged to the Columbia Jewish Congregation, which agreed to share space with the St. John the Baptist Catholic Church. Other congregations using the building had affairs in other halls, but used the same reception area. I liked all that intermingling. We even held some shared events.

Not everyone agreed. Some religious groups looked for and found out-parcels of real estate not owned by Rouse. Reaching those out-parcels took extra travel time for congregants, but they were willing to take the time rather than be bound by Rouse's covenants. Nonetheless, the Interfaith Centers still stand, and a good number of congregations, including the Columbia Jewish Congregation, still try to make them work. My former congregation is active, expanding, and well.

I imagine that the Columbia covenants made the various congregations aware and appreciative of each other. So, I think, perhaps even covenants without an enforcement protocol could be useful for promoting brotherhood or at least mutual appreciation.

I found a brotherhood formula that fit this mold fairly well. I noticed it inside the Jewish *Alenu* prayer, which has been around a long time. Some people believe it was authored by Joshua, the successor to Moses. Others think it was composed by a Talmudic giant, Abba Arika, familiarly known as "The Rav," who lived in Babylonia in the third century. Today, the prayer comes near the end of the standard daily Jewish religious service.

The *Alenu* is neither a prescription nor a covenant; like most Hebrew prayers, it is more like a poetic sketch, so that you can interpret it in a variety of ways. I formulated an interpretation of the relevant parts:

> It is incumbent upon us to praise the Master of the Universe and to recognize his grand creation . . . It is written in the Torah, "Know this day and consider it in your heart that the Lord is God in Heaven and on earth; there is no other God to consider."
>
> We therefore hope and trust, O Lord our God, that we may soon become fully aware of your glory and might, so that, working together with you, we will remove negative and idolatrous behavior from our earth. We hope for the day when the world will be perfected under your kingdom and all mankind will call upon your name . . . May it become perfectly

clear to all the habitants of the world that, before you, their knees must bend and their tongue vow loyalty. Before you, O Lord our God, may they bow in worship, giving honor to your glorious name.

May all of us accept the legitimacy of your kingdom and may you rule over us speedily and forever. For the kingdom is yours, and to all eternity you will reign in glory . . . as it has been foretold: "The Lord shall be King over all the earth. On that day, the Lord shall be one, and his name shall be one."

Even with my interpretation, the *Alenu* is short on specifics. Basically I hear it propose that if we all live right and follow our noblest inclinations, then God will embrace us as a single human family that lives as equals under his sovereignty.

Of course, the *Alenu* doesn't provide a signature line that commits everyone to comply. On the contrary, the *Alenu* raises questions about its universality in that, like other Jewish prayers, it refers to the "chosenness" of the Jewish people.

Modern Jews generally interpret this formulation to mean that we are "chosen for service to God," not chosen because God loves us better. We are chosen because God demands more of us, and that is reflected in the very title, *Alenu,* which means: "It is incumbent upon *us.* " Anyone can do it, but it is incumbent upon *us* because we are chosen for God's service. It is our *obligation;* it is everyone else's option.

However, I must admit that some Jews, especially those chafing personally under Christian persecution, don't like to include people of other religions in the *Alenu* or any other prayer. Hermann Cohen, the great German-Jewish philosopher, said he once found a cantor weeping after delivering the Yom Kippur prayers, which contain a passage that goes, "For My house shall be called a house of prayer for all the nations."

When asked why that passage made him cry, the cantor answered,

"How shall I not weep when the House of our Holiness shall be filled with *goyim?*" That cantor certainly wouldn't like a universalist interpretation of the *Alenu!*

Overcoming that resistance and voluntarily putting our signatures under the *Alenu* will be a big step toward achieving my Vision of Love.

How We Can Support Each Other

Christians and Jews don't have to wait until the day when rabbis, ministers, and priests join together to put their "John Hancock" under the *Alenu* or some other document with more specifics. We can benefit right now, each by observing how the other religion makes the God connection and adopting the best of it.

For a long time, Jewish worship communities, especially Orthodox ones, have resisted opening a window to the outside. Recently, however, rabbis became aware that staying closed to outside ideas means losing a valuable opportunity.

For example, Rabbi Joshua Gutoff, a faculty member of the (Orthodox) Academy for Jewish Religion, wrote an exhortative article in the June 3, 2002, issue of the *Jerusalem Report,* titled "Depend on the Knowledge of Strangers," He wrote,

"At its most rigorous, [Orthodox] insistence [on closing themselves off from the outside] becomes a complete rejection of the 'non-Torah' world.

The impulse is not limited, though, to the ultra-Orthodox community. Jews who feel completely at ease in secular culture have still been heard to say that they (non-Jewish congregations) have nothing to teach us about what is right, true, or good.

To encourage Jewish groups to open up to adaptation, Rabbi Gutoff points to the fact that even Torah supports adopting good ideas from the outside world. He points to Numbers 10:31, for example, where Moses asks his father-in-law, Jethro, to be his "guide" in adopting ideas from his different Midianite culture. Rabbi Gut-off exclaims, "Moses, the greatest of the prophets, is unashamedly asking for help!"

Until recently, Jewish worship deprived itself of the light and color that typify Christian devotion. Light and color were dropped from Jewish observance after the destruction of the Second Temple in the year 70. The dejection caused by that loss worsened after the Holocaust.

Before the destruction of the Temple, joyful music recounted in Psalm 150 used to suffuse Jewish services, as the New International Version (NIV) Bible translation proves.

Psalm 150

Praise him with the sounding of the trumpet,
Praise him with the harp and lyre,
Praise him with timbrel and dancing,
Praise him with the strings and pipe,
Praise him with the clash of cymbals . . .

I applaud Jewish congregations who want to recover the music, the dance, the joy, and the ecstasy in that psalm, which was maintained so effectively in Christian services. Putting back instrumental music into Jewish Services began in Germany during the late 1770s, the time of the *Haskalah,* or Jewish Enlightenment. Music that the Christians had preserved was adopted back into Jewish services. Some Reform temples in Germany even built organs that rivaled those in famous old cathedrals.

Other musical experiments have flourished in the practices of movements like Jewish Renewal, to which I belong. We have enlivened religious services with guitars, drums, and other instruments mentioned in Psalm 150.

An even newer adoption, spearheaded by my friend Sharon Alexander, uses Gospel music with Jewish themes. This spirited type of singing originally spread from African-American congregations to white churches, and now it is hopping into Jewish practice as "Jospel!"

I attended a "Jospel" event recently at the huge, mainstream B'nai Israel Congregation in Boca Raton, Florida. They invited a gospel choir from the nearby Ebenezer Baptist Church to sing with the Jewish choir to assure that the presentation sounded authentic. The response at the synagogue was enthusiastic; the whole place was a-rocking and a-rolling like true Baptists.

Innovations have flowed not only from Christian practice to the Jews, but also vice versa, as in observing the "New Year of the Trees." Known by Jews as the ancient holiday of *Tu B'shevat,* it derives from a Biblical directive in Leviticus 19:23–25 that fruit may not be harvested from a tree during the first three years of its life.

Tu B'shevat is declared the "birth date" of fruit tree plantings for the entire year, so that fruit is deemed kosher to eat once a tree has reached its third *Tu B'shevat. (Shevat* is a month in the Hebrew calendar roughly corresponding to January. The prefix *Tu* stands for the number fifteen, because Hebrew uses letters for numbers as in the Roman system, where the Fourth of July would be written as "the IV of July.")

Neither Jews nor Christians paid much attention to the Biblical institution of *Tu B'shevat* until the date was elevated by the increasing interest in environmental conservation especially of orchards, parks, and forests. In addition, *Tu B'shevat* gained appeal as holiday to fill the gap in the Jewish observation calendar between Chanukah in December and Purim in March. The Christian calendar has the same gap between Christmas in December and Palm Sunday in March.

Jewish innovators gradually developed a service for *Tu B'shevat* patterned after the Passover Seder. This further appeals to Christians because of their increased awareness of the link between Passover and Easter.

A word of caution here: Religious communities mainly experience success with elements from another religious practice if the motivation behind it is spiritual. If it's just a fad, it loses its core value and shows its dross.

Take, for example, the recently popularized and commercially promoted study of Kabbalah. The Kabbalah used to be reserved to Jewish mystics over forty, but now it has become modish. Kabbalistic practices have become embedded in our culture, and there is no turning back.

Less embedded, but more lamentable, is the so-called *Faux Bar Mitzvah*. The *Baltimore Jewish Times* described such an event (Simchas Section, February 29, 2008, pp. 26–27).

It said:

A *faux bar mitzvah* is a party thrown by non-Jewish parents for their children to experience the same coming-of-age event given Jewish boys.

They may serve a challah, light candles, or dance a *horah* . . . but few other Jewish traditions exist on the agenda.

This lack of spiritual content has also backfired on Jewish celebrations. Critics call it "focusing on the *bar* (referring to the copious serving of liquor in English) instead of the *mitzvah* (meaning "religious duty" in Hebrew)."

Rabbi Elissa Sachs-Kohen of Baltimore Hebrew Congregation pointed that out in an article, also published in the *Baltimore Jewish Times*. She said:

It makes sense that 13-year-olds focus on the party, but I hope adults can give them a larger perspective. I'd say to a non-Jewish [parent], "You think it's so wonderful? I do, too."

But I'd get them involved in . . . the process of engaging with their own tradition. That's the part worth emulating.

Of course it depends on one's point of view whether an adaptation is an improvement. I already have mentioned that I don't like infusing the "Christmas spirit" into Chanukah. Some people may applaud it, but I think we Jews took it from Christianity without adding much value. I shudder at the silly imitation Christmas lights, the inappropriate Christmas gifts, the copycat Christmas cards, the ironically named Chanukah bush. Chanukah isn't Christmas, and it can't and shouldn't be elevated to a major holiday.

I can wail about it all I want, but it doesn't help. Now that the Chanukmas reindeer has escaped from Pandora's box, it can't be put back inside.

How We Can Enhance Prayer Together

Christians and Jews can go beyond enhancing each other's worship; we can also join together to enhance the basic efficacy of prayer. Congregations of all stripes are seeing attendance drop. Those of us who see value in prayer can profitably work together in reexamining its elements to make prayer more attractive and more accessible to more people.

Prayer as a practice is relatively new for both Christians and Jews. Up until the time that the proto-Christians came along, we Jews had been communicating with God mainly by means of (mostly animal) sacrifice done according to a precise, cultic procedure. When the Temple in Jerusalem was destroyed in 70 AD, the practice of sacrifice was destroyed along with it. In that same era, Proto-Christians were starting to formulate their own practices and, along with mainstream Jews, started to develop prayer as a substitute for animal sacrifice.

Rather than pursuing precisely how the practice of prayer developed, I would like to examine seven aspects of prayer that strike me as significant and see how each could be strengthened. These elements are:

- **The motives** that move us to pray
- **The lack of realism** in the wording
- **The repetitiveness** of the words
- **The frequency** of calls to prayer
- **The length** of typical prayer service
- **The locations** used for prayer, and
- **The efficacy** of prayer.

The motives that move us to pray aren't all that different from what motivated our forebears to conduct animal sacrifice. At first, the Torah discussions on this topic sounds strange to modern ears. Some passages seem to indicate that God likes the presentation of a good juicy steak and appreciates the "savory smoke" that ascends from a steak roast at the Temple. However, in its more psychologically astute passages, Torah repeats with emphasis that the sacrifice is not "for" God but for the person bringing the sacrifice. The person making the sacrifice has breached a God-made commandment and makes the sacrifice to "fess up" and to promise to do better.

I see value in moral accounting and penitent prayer. Still, I think we should examine when we pray whether we want to atone or whether we just want to wiggle into God's good graces. While our forebears might have employed sacrifice to ingratiate themselves by sending up "savory smoke," we moderns might be trying to do the same with savory remarks.

Sure, we can and should make personal pleas to God to deal with pain, sorrow, and loss; at the same time, I believe we also should avoid the belief that God will grant us favors just because we're asking "so nicely."

The lack of realism in the wording of some prayers is readily apparent. One prayer that really challenges me is the *Amidah*, the high point of our God connection. Because of its centrality, I don't want to skip it, but I trip over its unrealistic wording. It affirms that "God restores life to the dead, lifts up the fallen, heals the sick, sets free the captives, and keeps faith with those who sleep in the dust."

I think to myself, *Didn't the author of this prayer notice that our cemeteries are full of unrisen dead, our hospitals are full of the fallen and the sick, our jails are full of captives, and our cities are full of homeless people who sleep in the dust?*

My congregation uses a new prayer book in which the author has carefully substituted new words, see *Siddur Eit Ratzon* by Joseph G. Rosenstein, (Shiviti Publications, Highland Park, New Jersey, 2006). Rosenstein's rational solution reflects his profession; he teaches mathematics at Rutgers University. With regard to the *Amidah*, he says (on pp. 167 and 168):

[We have particular] problems with the concept of life after death [and] the notion of God as all-powerful, of which "giving life to the dead" is but one example. God's power was not manifest during the Holocaust, or on September 11, or at other times in the history of our people and of the world when divine intervention would have made a difference.

"It seems impossible to maintain at the same time that God is powerful and that God is good, unless we abandon our rationality . . . [My perspective is that,] to make room for human choice, God withdraws from micromanaging the universe and lets the world continue without divine intervention.

Therefore, we offer here the alternative of speaking of God's *presence* rather than God's *power*. God is always present, always with us, providing us with strength and comfort, guidance and dignity.

Another way I deal with this anomaly is deeming the word choice metaphoric. I see the *Amidah* prayer enabling us to face to death with dignity, deal humanely with the incarcerated, and respond generously to those in need of decent housing. That's not just Ami-chai's idea; that's what prophet after prophet has been drumming into our dear little ears, from Moses to Isaiah: "Justice, justice shalt thou pursue."

Even so, my literal ears still find seemingly unrealistic prayer disturbing. My late wife, Helene Hirschler, had her own response to this dilemma. She used to say, "Prayers aren't meant to convey meaning. They are mantras meant to enhance spirituality. The spirit of the prayer should lift you up from ordinary consciousness to a higher level."

In that spirit, when the prayer leader announces the start of the *Amidah,* I stop focusing on the words altogether, and I zone out to another level of consciousness.

The repetitiveness of the words in prayer sometimes bore me so much that I stay away from formal prayer altogether. I wonder, *"Does all of that repetitive wording really provide a vibrant connection with God?"*

An extreme example is the Kaddish, in essence a prayer of praise for God, which comes in six versions using the entire prayer or key parts of it. The most frequently repeated version is recited in remem-brance of a deceased relative. It is recited up to six times during a morning service, and twice during the afternoon and evening ser-vice, for a total of ten times each day.

Three other versions recur during special occasions. The "Whole Kaddish" is recited after the conclusion of major sections of prayer services, and the "Half Kaddish" indicates the conclusion of minor sections. The Kaddish-D'Rabannan (Rabbis' Kaddish)is reserved for the Rabbi and the Kaddish-D'Itchad'ta, for concluding study of major tractates of Talmud.

Father Anthony Lusvardi, SJ responded to a question critiquing repetitive prayer (in a blog on Ignatianspirituality.com). He said:

A thoughtful undergraduate here at Loyola . . . criticized

. . . repeating the same prayers over and over again, being needlessly redundant in prayer, failing to be spontaneous enough, just using the same words again and again in repetition without coming up with anything new—much like this sentence.

The previous poorly written sentence demonstrates, however, that one can be redundant even without repeating the same phrases, . . . but in prayer, perhaps, redundancy isn't any great fault . . . Prayer isn't primarily about exchanging information.

Prayer is, however, about communication. One reason to communicate is, yes, to exchange information, but another is to build relationships . . . [For] example, [take] the deeply philosophical conversations I have with my eight-month-old niece Chloe . . .

I repeat phrases like "Oh, Chloe, you are the cutest baby" over and over again, and she blows spit bubbles in reply.

I could just as well be speaking Klingon, and it wouldn't diminish the quality of the communication, because what's important in these exchanges is not really verbal. My baby talk is just an excuse to be together, a way of showing affection. I would maintain that important communication is happening nonetheless, despite a lack of verbal content. Chloe, after all, smiles and laughs, and I would rather listen to her spit bubbles than just about any other conversation . . .

In relationships, some things are so important that they bear repeating. A husband might tell his wife, "I love you," every day before going to work, but the fact that the phrase has become, in a sense, ritualized doesn't diminish its power or meaning. Some things are so true that they should be repeated.

I actually know a woman who complains that her husband doesn't tell her often enough that he loves her. In my marriage, I probably err in the other direction. I talk a lot about love, and sometimes my wife wonders whether I do so because of fear that I may lose her.

Therefore, I think that not expressing love to God may mean love has flown out the window. On the other hand, excessive declarations of love, may be motivated by the fear that unless we do it over and over, God may disconnect and leave us exposed to a horrid fate. With this in mind, repetition is well worth discussing by congregations who want to rethink repetition in their prayer practice.

The frequency of calls to prayer by many faith communities seems over-lavish. In the case of us Jews, tradition requires group prayer each morning, afternoon, and evening.

To examine whether frequency of contact with God makes sense, I will put it side by side with my staying connected with my friend Dave Alkire, a faithful friend since we roomed together at Ohio State University in Columbus. These days I telephone Dave once or twice per month, but not with any precise regularity; he'd consider it odd if I did.

Now imagine what would happen if I set up a conference call to him with nine other friends three times a day to parallel the way we Jews assemble at least a quorum of ten for a thrice daily group prayer to God.

Once I started a ritual like that, Dave would quickly send for men in white coats to take me to the Funny Farm. Perhaps the comparison seems silly, but I truly wonder whether God really appreciates all those conference calls, all that chatter.

Part of the answer may lie in Talmudic lore that suggests God actually likes a good chat. It says that God created humans because God was lonely. Just as human friends maintain friendship with verbal communication, so people who appreciate God maintain their relationship through prayer.

That logic makes sense, but I still ask, "Why so often?" People who are truly comfortable with themselves and one another don't need to keep talking endlessly. We all know couples who have happily grown old together. They now say little, because each knows that their partners loves them, values them, and cares about them. After four thousand years (or more) of living in communion with our God, do we still need to incessantly send up words, words, words?

We might not need any words at all. Mystics have said that all of creation does not stop praying naturally. The moon's golden glow in a dark sky is the moon's prayer. The fragrance spread into the air is a flower's prayer.

Mystics then draw the parallel with humans, whom they see as praying just by breathing. However, unlike the other creatures, we humans possess a conscious mind, and breathing silently doesn't register in the same way as words do. Only if we pause purposefully, take a deep breath, savor it completely, and let it out with a sense of gratitude would breathing be more like praying.

Controlled breathing is central to effective meditation, and I strongly recommend it. (I'm working on a book to enable it, tentatively called *Meditation—Jewish Style*.) Meditation then becomes a way to make our breathing into silent prayer. However, with all we moderns have to do, controlled breathing isn't practical to do twenty-four seven.

We can, however, practice mindful living. Jewish masters encourage it. They say that an ordinary act like eating can turn from routine to holy if we mindfully pray at the dining table. It brings a life-giving but automatic activity into clear awareness.

Broadening out this reasoning, regular prayers can consistently vivify our sense of being alive and express gratitude for this. Regarded this way, frequent prayer starts making more sense. Therefore, faith communities might make prayer more meaningful by concentrating on mindfulness, instead of mindless repetition.

The length of a typical prayer service reminds me of a principle by my teachers in effective writing: *"If you can say it in three words, don't use a dozen."*

The typical Jewish service lasts so long, I get itchy feet. First comes the recital of Psalms. Fortunately, I've never had to sit through a recital of all 150 of them but still the my standard Conservative *Sabbath and Festival Prayer Book* uses Psalms 29, 92, 93, 95, 96, 97, 98, and 99. Eight Psalms! No digests! In every single evening service! Necessary? Oh, really!

Catholics do it far better; they keep each mass to exactly an hour, including the sermon.

My congregation in Baltimore saw my impatience, and agreed to limit Psalm reading to a line or two from each of the standard eight, stressing the main theme.

Even "routine blessings" said as we move through our regular day can be overlong. I'm looking at what I call the "Bathroom Prayer," because we say it, among other occasions, after using the toilet.

The standard version contains all of these many words (in translation from the Hebrew):

Blessed are You, our Lord, King of the Universe, who created humans in wisdom and has placed within them openings and closings, pipes and conduits. The facts, evidenced before Your glorious throne, reveal that if but one of these opened improperly, or if but one of them was blocked, it would be impossible for people to survive and stand up in your world. Blessed are You, O Lord, healer of mankind, who does wondrous things.

By the time I utter all those words after leaving the bathroom, I'm almost ready to start a second session on the toilet!

To bypass all that repetition, I have shortened this prayer using the pattern of the Evening Twilight prayer, which I particularly like. I succinctly say: "Blessed are You, Our God and King of the Universe, who opens up pipes and conduits, in their proper time, according to Your will."

I don't want to totally do away with the original, because the Jewish Master who composed it obviously thought every single word was appropriate. I am reminded of a scene in the movie *Amadeus,* where the Duke says he doesn't like Mozart's new composition.

"Why not?" Mozart asks.

"Too many notes," the Duke answers.

Undaunted, Mozart remarks, "Your Excellency, the number of notes I used is exactly right for this piece."

Perhaps the author of the Bathroom Prayer agreed with Mozart, so I am open to discovering more inspiration from the original. I can visualize myself standing before my Lord, Healer of Mankind, and be amazed at all the wondrous gifts he placed in this world. The approach validates the oft-used Hebrew motto, "Know before Whom you stand."

The locations used for prayer are generally indoors, away from nature. On my way to synagogue, psalter in hand, I sometime ask myself: *Why do we need a building to effectively commune with God?* Sure, praying from a book in a synagogue beats sipping beer in a bar or playing bingo in the basement, but is it really the only good place for it? Is there no congregation that meets on a beach?

My answer to these questions came on a lovely spring morning when I went to the seashore at Deerfield Beach, Florida, for an early morning meditation. As I topped the little rise between the sidewalk and the beach, I saw a small group of people in prayer shawls and hats, so of course I asked what they were doing. A tall woman introduced herself as the cantor of Temple Beth Orr in Coral Springs. She said a group of them comes to the beach each year on the last day of Passover for a special sunrise ceremony.

"I'm glad I came at the right time," I said.

"More than you know," she answered. "There was a glitch in our synagogue announcements, and only a few of us heard that the ceremony is today. We're nine, you're the tenth, and so now we have enough people for a *minyan,* to start prayers in a quorum."

I enjoyed the ceremony and since then I have called Temple Beth Orr "My Beach Congregation."

Since then, I have found other congregations sometimes have group prayers at the beach and I've found that out there, in nature, spirituality floods in and the content ebbs in importance.

That still leaves open the question that if you can pray any place at all, why build costly prayer halls so we can do most of our prayers in a building? Torah Scripture seems to suggest that during our 40 years of wandering in the desert, God actually met us in person when we prayed in our portable Tabernacle.

Whether that was literally true doesn't matter; prayer vibes build up inside a dedicated space, thereby inviting more of the same. A group of dedicated worshipers can form a circle, metaphorically or actually, that lets God in. God can become part of our life in that setting, enrich our sense of belonging to an orderly, God-loving world.

Since both indoor and outdoor locales have their advantage for prayer, I live on the beach and I pray there when I can, and I also enjoy services with friends inside convenient indoor spaces!

The efficacy of prayer is hard to nail down. People who stay away from prayer services may think, *If it doesn't get me anything, why do it?*

I considered this question in an inspirational dream:

I am at a convention of flower shop owners, and it's my job to introduce the keynote speaker. He is a flower exporter from Israel.

I get on stage, greet the audience, and say some kind words about the speaker. I relate that he tends a vegetable garden and a small flock of chickens, but that his main interest, of course, is exporting flowers from Israel. He told me that he has no prepared text; he will just answer questions.

Right away, a hand goes up from the rear of the room. The questioner speaks in rapid-fire Hebrew, and the invited speaker answers in rapid-fire Hebrew. No one else, including me, understands the exchange, and it is so unexpected that people start laughing in surprise.

I think the speaker from Israel in the dream is a representative of

God. (Whether he is an angel or Jesus depends on which tradition you follow; on the dreaming level, it doesn't matter.) The speaker tells me of his humble activities (a little garden, a little flock) to show that he is close to us humans and our concerns. His main concern, however, is love (flowers from Israel).

The dream tells me that we humans may want to query God about the effectiveness of prayer, but we falter from the get-go because we can't word the question understandably. Much less can we comprehend the reply when God's answers come.

The significance of prayer, therefore, lies in the ecstasy, not in the words. If we pray right, we can float down a stream that carries along everything, from distant stars, to human beings, to fireflies. Since God is One, God is in that very stream of Everything.

In sum, the dream says that, instead of intellectualizing, we can sit in love together. Love and laugh together—that seems to be God's suggestion for building a lasting congregation that supports my Vision of Love.

The Road from Enmity to Love

In the last few decades, relations between Christians and Jews have improved. Catholic officials and theologians have acknowledged the horror of the Inquisition, and have apologized to survivors and their offspring who still suffer from its aftereffects.

One voice that spoke out with a ringing effect, belongs to Joseph Ratzinger. In 1997, he spoke as the head of the Congregation for the Doctrine of the Faith, the current successor agency to the Office of the Inquisition. His voice rang out even louder after he was elected Pope Benedict XVI. People took notice when he publicly declared, "I consider this [Inquisition] a sin that should make us reflect and lead us to repentance."

The Catholic Church has gone beyond trying to blot out the stain on its name from the Inquisition. In a positive outreach to today, Jews, the Pope proclaimed that Christians and Jews ought now to be engaged in "prudence and love." That's the expression used in *Nostra Aetate,* which I cited before and which is reprinted in full in Appendix A.

Further along, the document states:

> The Church, therefore, exhorts her sons, that through dialogue and collaboration with the followers of other religions, carried out with prudence and love and in witness to the Christian faith and life, they recognize, preserve and promote the good things, spiritual and moral, as well as the socio-cultural values found among these men. . .
>
> No foundation therefore remains for any theory or practice that leads to discrimination between man and man or people and people, so far as their human dignity and the rights flowing from it are concerned.

It may seem simplistic to say that all pitfalls in relationships between Christians and Jews can be avoided with "prudence and love." Yet, properly applied, love does help us build bridges. We can approach these bridges from both sides and meet in the middle. Today we drive automobiles along superhighways without even realizing that, on our way, we cross physical bridges built years ago. I hope for the day that we will cross spiritual bridges as easily.

At present, each religious community in the world drives its own process toward God along its own road, and what's missing is access to each other's road. We see just a piece of our brotherhood as humans who worship God.

We act just like the blind men in the fable who experience only a piece of an elephant. Using their hands instead of their eyes, each blind man notices an important part of the elephant without getting any sense of what the entire elephant is like. One man feels a leg and thinks he's embracing a pillar; another fingers a trunk and believes it's a garden hose; and so on.

The story illustrates that by exchanging information on what they feel with their fingers, the blind men could form a pretty accurate picture of the animal. Even though God certainly is more complex than an elephant, our several faith communities, each reaching out from its own stance, has an important aspect of God in its grip.

We worshipers of various faiths can and should communicate. We can use our gift of speech to share our individual experiences and thereby discover that our various forms of worship are all part of a coherent whole because all prayer is directed at the same source.

If we connect spirituality with our Maker, do you think He cares if you prayed to him as a Unitary God or as a Golden Calf? The God I visualize judges prayer by its sincerity, not by its form of address.

The Talmud tells the story of Honi, the rainmaker (also known as Honi, the Circle Drawer), who earned fame for being able to successfully pray for rain. (See Mishnah Ta'anit 3:8.)

On one occasion, God was slow to respond, so Honi drew a circle in the dust and informed God that he would not move until God would send down rain as requested.

God responded with a drizzle, and Honi told God he wanted a heavier rain. Then it began to pour, and Honi said: "Please God, not that hard. I want a calm rain," and the rain diminished till Honi was satisfied.

If the Talmud accedes to Honi's praying to Adonai as the God of Rainstorms, it proves to me that you can pray to God in any capacity of His.

At bottom, religiousness as a concept overshadows the practices of any specific religion. Each religion has aspects that bolster us in prayer and strengthen our faith. In prayer, we all are alike, and the spiritual ends we strive for are the same.

Yes, sure, I pray to a Unitary God, not to a Universe of gods, because I was brought up by a religious Jew, my Uncle Max. However, I also was brought up in part by my Catholic foster family that protected me during the Nazi era. I can pray either way.

When we bring—literally—common sense to our connection with God, we will be well on our way toward my Vision of Love.

Achieving Reciprocity

Yes, one group did reach out in response, the Institute for Christians and Jewish Studies, but they don't speak for any of the umbrella agencies of established Jewish worship groups.

The institute is an independent, educational non-profit organization composed of various authorities on Christian and Jewish interrelations. It is located in my hometown of Baltimore, and I know them from following their website and from conversations with its Executive Director, Dr. Christopher Leighton. (The Institute recently added Moslem scholars to its fold and adjusted its name to "The Institute for Islamic, Christian and Jewish Studies.)

After considerable internal debate and discussion, the Institute published a formal document titled *Dabru Emet* ("Speak of Truth), and subtitled, "A Jewish Statement on Christians and Christianity."

The introduction to the document states:

An increasing number of official Church bodies, both Roman Catholic and Protestant, have made public statements of their remorse about Christian mistreatment of Jews and Judaism. These statements have declared, furthermore, that Christian teaching and preaching can and must be reformed so that they acknowledge God's enduring covenant with the Jewish people and celebrate the contribution of Judaism to world civilization and to Christian faith itself.

We believe these changes merit a thoughtful Jewish response. Speaking only for ourselves—an interdenominational group of Jewish scholars—we believe it is time for Jews to learn about the efforts of Christians to honor Judaism. We believe it is time for Jews to reflect on what Judaism may now say about Christianity.

I personally want to follow these suggestions. I have detailed the numerous visions and exhortations pushing me to feel love for Christians in a way that fully encompasses their religious beliefs. I have endeavored to express my love without reservation.

Even though I feel pushed to my limits, I still feel vestiges of resentment deep within myself, left over from a truckload of pain caused by two millennia of persecution.

On top of that load, my back rises up like that of an imperiled cat when I feel the huge discrepancy in our numbers: An overwhelming 2 billion rather assertive Christians on this earth, confronting a mere 12 million rather meek Jews.

Rome wasn't built in a day, nor was Jerusalem. I have every hope and expectation that I will eventually reach the position of unconditional love that author and speaker Caroline Myss talks about. I'll also learn to fully appreciate hearing from Christians that they recognize and repent their part in the two millennia of persecution that we Jews have undergone.

I have traveled a great distance from being a Child of the Holocaust to a promoter of love for Christians, and I give myself credit for it. As I mentioned, I discovered that to be a good lover of Christians, I first have to be a good Jew, and I have consciously strengthened my Jewish knowledge and intensified my practice. I have traveled the internal and external roads that lead to appreciating the faith of the other. I recognize the deep spiritual longing and heartfelt devotion of Christians, and I understand how they reach it through their tie to Jesus.

So I'm communicating with my fellow Jews through my Vision of Love to share that understanding with you. I urge you to be receptive when Christians reach out to us. If our minds, hearts, and souls aren't open, we'll fail to see the outstretched hand when it is being extended.

The Jewish scholars on the committee that responded to the Pope's *Nostra Aetate* offer eight specific statements to help Jews and Christians relate better (see the full text of *Dabru Emet* in Appendix B).

Even that noble beginning is hard for us Jews to accept, and most rabbis have not signed onto it. The reservations Jews express towards the carefully crafted *Dabru Emet* came to the fore during the 2008 "Colloqium on the Scandal of Particularity" held in Richmond, Virginia, in March 2008 (I saw it reported in the ICJS quarterly newsletter of Spring 2008, called *"In A Word,"* page 7.)

Dr. Adam Gregerman, one of the ICJS Jewish scholars, attended and then reviewed the 2008 Colloquium, and reported:

> It was highly significant and not a little unsettling, for Jews to hear Christians asking them [Jews] to consider their [Christian] views of their religious legitimacy vis-a-vis the God of Israel. Some Jewish participants in Richmond struggled to respond in ways that both demonstrated thoughtful consideration of their Christian friends' requests, while nonetheless recognizing the overall lack of guidance offered for such a request in the Jewish tradition.
>
> First, Jews have long thought of humanity dichotomously, divided into Israel and the Nations. The Christian request potentially undermines this traditional division.
>
> Second, Jews have historically expressed little interest in Christianity per se . . . . Theologically if not politically, they viewed Christianity much as they viewed other religions—perhaps deprecating them but largely seeing them as fundamentally irrelevant to their covenant with God . . . .
>
> There may be ways for Jews to recognize some distinctive status for Christians—perhaps through adaptation of the idea of the Righteous Gentiles [a term invented to describe Christians who saved Jews during the Holocaust) . . . I believe all relationships require both Jews and Christians to strive to see others as others see themselves, and to give some account of how we ourselves see those others.

As I indicated, my knees get a bit shaky when challenged, similar to what the participants in the Colloquium at Richmond expressed. My knees, however, are becoming sturdier and steadier. They have been strengthened by the experience of meeting Christians like Joy Smith who are firm in their Christianity and are happy to share it without any expectations from me.

I have met other sincere Christians who seek us out without deviating from their own faith, like Pastor Frank Eiklor. I met him during a seminar on interfaith relations several years ago, and we keep in touch via the internet. In the same newsletter I mentioned earlier, *Shalom International* (December 1, 2007), he presented his consistent stance of unconditional love toward Jews. He said:

> I [have] declared that Christians who call for a *quid pro quo* support from Jewish leaders are not in line with Jesus. Some evangelicals told Jews, "We will support you if you support us."
>
> This is not what Scripture teaches. You and I are to stand with Jews and Israel (and anyone else) in their pain, whether or not they return to us kind words or actions. It's called 'unconditional love'—and it means just that.
>
> One thing I know, the more intimately one loves the Son of God, the more we will love the apple of God's eye—Israel and the Jewish people. His compassion for the physical family of Abraham, Isaac, and Jacob is woven throughout Scripture from Genesis through Revelation.

Some Christian friends with whom I discussed Judaism have even delved into the beauty of Judaism—not with any thought of converting, but with a motivation to learn. Through this study they have come to love both the Jewish lore of yore and the Jewish people of today. They have come to appreciate my idea that Jewish practice contains elements that can assist Christians in deepening their own faith.

I see a good portent when I look at the paragraph preceding the cardboard division between the Jewish Bible and the Christian New Testament in my unified copy of "The Holy Scriptures."

The final Old Testament verse begins: "Look! I am sending to you people Elijah the Prophet before the coming of the great and fear-inspiring day of God."

To me, "the great and fear-inspiring day of God" is the day we realize my Vision of Love. A shift in attitude is needed to get that snowball rolling. I know that the snowball can't be forced to happen; it can't be commanded or even cajoled. Yet, on rose-colored mornings, I see the dawn of a day when Jews are lovingly opening to Christians, and the cardboard division between our two testaments crumbles.

Jewish teachings already exist with the right attitude, even though they weren't formulated in order to reach out to Christians. For example, I am heartened by the words of Rabbi Yehuda Leib HaLevi Ashlag (1884–1954), who interpreted Kabbalah to promote unity.

He is popularly known as the Baal HaSulam (Owner of the Ladder) for his ladderized commentary on *The Book of Zohar,* and he is one of the few old-line kabbalists from Poland who escaped the Holocaust. I noticed his reasoning when I saw a quote from his works on a wall plaque at the Tel Aviv Museum of Art. It says:

> While pointing at the precept, "Love your neighbor as your-self," Kabbalah wishes to say that the entire universe was created according to this law. Only, our world is functioning in accordance with the opposite property: "Love for oneself." If man in this world wishes to exist in harmony with the general law of the universe, he is bound to change and adapt himself to it. The cause of all suffering in the world lies in our opposition to this general law.

His point is that natural law supports the precept of loving your neighbor. If you want a better world, then love your neighbor. If you'd rather bear grudges, don't be surprised if you make the world fall apart.

A modern-day Torah discussion makes the same point even more dramatically. The discussion takes off from the opening paragraphs of the Talmud, which deal with deciding when night arrives after dusk and when morning begins after dawn. At first blush, it appears to be a light topic with which to start weighty discussions, but when you think about it, the topic is a practical one. If you want to know when it's time for your morning prayers, you have to have a way for deciding when "morning" has arrived.

One respected rabbi used this topic to point his students into the direction of brotherly love. He asked them to imagine how they themselves would go about determining when night has ended and a new day has dawned. (From *Tales of Chasidim*, quoted in *Touching the Holy* by Robert J. Wicks, Ave Maria Press, 1992.)

> A student suggested: Could it be one when you can see an animal in the distance and can tell whether it's a sheep or a dog?"
>
> "No," said the rabbi. A few more students suggested differentiating a fig tree from a pear tree and similar distinctions. They all weren't right, the rabbi said.
>
> "So then, you tell us," the students said.
>
> The Rabbi pronounced: "It is when you can look on the face of a person and see that it is your sister or brother. If you can't see that, it is still night."

Appendix A.
Nostra Aetate

Declaration on the Relation of the Church
to Non-Christian Religions

An Encyclical Promulgated on October 28, 1965,
by Pope Paul VI

A Proclamation by the Vatican

In our time, when day by day mankind is being drawn closer together,
and the ties between different peoples are becoming stronger, the
Church examines more closely the relationship to non-Christian
religions. In her task of promoting unity and love among men,
indeed among nations, she considers above all in this declaration
what men have in common and what draws them to fellowship.

One is the community of all peoples, one their origin, for God
made the whole human race to live over the face of the earth. One
also is their final goal, God. His providence, His manifestations of
goodness, His saving design extend to all men, until that time when
the elect will be united in the Holy City, the city ablaze with the
glory of God, where the nations will walk in His light.

Men expect from the various religions answers to the unsolved
riddles of the human condition, which today, even as in former
times, deeply stir the hearts of men: What is man? What is the
meaning, the aim of our life? What is moral good, what sin? Whence
suffering and what purpose does it serve? Which is the road to true

happiness? What are death, judgment and retribution after death? What, finally, is that ultimate inexpressible mystery which encompasses our existence: whence do we come, and where are we going?

From ancient times down to the present, there is found among various peoples a certain perception of that hidden power which hovers over the course of things and over the events of human history; at times some indeed have come to the recognition of a Supreme Being, or even of a Father. This perception and recognition penetrates their lives with a profound religious sense.

Religions, however, that are bound up with an advanced culture have struggled to answer the same questions by means of more refined concepts and a more developed language. Thus in Hinduism, men contemplate the divine mystery and express it through an inexhaustible abundance of myths and through searching philosophical inquiry. They seek freedom from the anguish of our human condition either through ascetic practices or profound meditation or a flight to God with love and trust. Again, Buddhism, in its various forms, realizes the radical insufficiency of this changeable world; it teaches a way by which men, in a devout and confident spirit, may be able either to acquire the state of perfect liberation, or attain, by their own efforts or through higher help, supreme illumination. Likewise, other religions found everywhere try to counter the restlessness of the human heart, each in its own manner, by proposing "ways," comprising teachings, rules of life, and sacred rites.

The Catholic Church rejects nothing that is true and holy in these religions. She regards with sincere reverence those ways of conduct and of life, those precepts and teachings which, though differing in many aspects from the ones she holds and sets forth, nonetheless often reflect a ray of that Truth which enlightens all men. Indeed, she proclaims, and ever must proclaim Christ "the way, the truth, and the life" (John 14:6), in whom men may find the fullness of religious life, in whom God has reconciled all things to Himself.

The Church, therefore, exhorts her sons, that through dialogue and collaboration with the followers of other religions, carried out with prudence and love and in witness to the Christian faith and life, they recognize, preserve and promote the good things, spiritual and moral, as well as the socio-cultural values found among these men.

The Church regards with esteem also the Moslems. They adore the one God, living and subsisting in Himself; merciful and all-powerful, the Creator of heaven and earth, who has spoken to men; they take pains to submit wholeheartedly to even His inscrutable decrees, just as Abraham, with whom the faith of Islam takes pleasure in linking itself, submitted to God.

Though they do not acknowledge Jesus as God, they revere Him as a prophet. They also honor Mary, His virgin Mother; at times they even call on her with devotion. In addition, they await the day of judgment when God will render their deserts to all those who have been raised up from the dead. Finally, they value the moral life and worship God especially through prayer, almsgiving and fasting.

Since in the course of centuries not a few quarrels and hostilities have arisen between Christians and Moslems, this sacred synod urges all to forget the past and to work sincerely for mutual understanding and to preserve as well as to promote together for the benefit of all mankind social justice and moral welfare, as well as peace and freedom.

As the sacred synod searches into the mystery of the Church, it remembers the bond that spiritually ties the people of the New Covenant to Abraham's stock.

Thus the Church of Christ acknowledges that, according to God's saving design, the beginnings of her faith and her election are found already among the Patriarchs, Moses and the prophets. She professes that all who believe in Christ—Abraham's sons according to faith—are included in the same Patriarch's call, and likewise that the salvation of the Church is mysteriously foreshadowed by the chosen people's exodus from the land of bondage.

The Church, therefore, cannot forget that she received the revelation of the Old Testament through the people with whom God in His inexpressible mercy concluded the Ancient Covenant. Nor can she forget that she draws sustenance from the root of that well-cultivated olive tree onto which have been grafted the wild shoots, the Gentiles. Indeed, the Church believes that by His cross Christ, Our Peace, reconciled Jews and Gentiles, making both one in Himself.

The Church keeps ever in mind the words of the Apostle about his kinsmen: "theirs is the sonship and the glory and the covenants and the law and the worship and the promises; theirs are the fathers and from them is the Christ according to the flesh" (Rom. 9:4–5), the Son of the Virgin Mary. She also recalls that the Apostles, the Church's mainstay and pillars, as well as most of the early disciples who proclaimed Christ's Gospel to the world, sprang from the Jewish people.

As Holy Scripture testifies, Jerusalem did not recognize the time of her visitation, nor did the Jews in large number, accept the Gospel; indeed not a few opposed its spreading. Nevertheless, God holds the Jews most dear for the sake of their Fathers; He does not repent of the gifts He makes or of the calls He issues-such is the witness of the Apostle. In company with the Prophets and the same Apostle, the Church awaits that day, known to God alone, on which all peoples will address the Lord in a single voice and "serve him shoulder to shoulder" (Soph. 3:9).

Since the spiritual patrimony common to Christians and Jews is thus so great, this sacred synod wants to foster and recommend that mutual understanding and respect which is the fruit, above all, of biblical and theological studies as well as of fraternal dialogues.

True, the Jewish authorities and those who followed their lead pressed for the death of Christ; still, what happened in His passion cannot be charged against all the Jews, without distinction, then alive, nor against the Jews of today. Although the Church is the new people of God, the Jews should not be presented as rejected or accursed by God, as if this followed from the Holy Scriptures. All should see to it, then, that in catechetical work or in the preaching of the word of God they do not teach anything that does not conform to the truth of the Gospel and the spirit of Christ.

Furthermore, in her rejection of every persecution against any man, the Church, mindful of the patrimony she shares with the Jews and moved not by political reasons but by the Gospel's spiritual love, decries hatred, persecutions, displays of anti-Semitism, directed against Jews at any time and by anyone.

Besides, as the Church has always held and holds now, Christ underwent His passion and death freely, because of the sins of men and out of infinite love, in order that all may reach salvation. It is, therefore, the burden of the Church's preaching to proclaim the cross of Christ as the sign of God's all-embracing love and as the fountain from which every grace flows.

We cannot truly call on God, the Father of all, if we refuse to treat in a brotherly way any man, created as he is in the image of God. Man's relation to God the Father and his relation to men his brothers are so linked together that Scripture says: "He who does not love does not know God" (1 John 4:8).

No foundation therefore remains for any theory or practice that leads to discrimination between man and man or people and people, so far as their human dignity and the rights flowing from it are concerned.

The Church reproves, as foreign to the mind of Christ, any discrimination against men or harassment of them because of their race, color, condition of life, or religion. On the contrary, following in the footsteps of the holy Apostles Peter and Paul, this sacred synod ardently implores the Christian faithful to "maintain good fellowship among the nations" (1 Peter 2:12), and, if possible, to live for their part in peace with all men, so that they may truly be sons of the Father who is in heaven.

Appendix B.
Dabru Emet

Jewish Statement on Christians and Christianity
Published by the National Jewish Scholars Project, September 10, 2000

In recent years, there has been a dramatic and unprecedented shift in Jewish and Christian relations. Throughout the nearly two millennia of Jewish exile, Christians have tended to characterize Judaism as a failed religion or, at best, a religion that prepared the way for, and is completed in, Christianity.

In the decades since the Holocaust, however, Christianity has changed dramatically. An increasing number of official Church bodies, both Roman Catholic and Protestant, have made public statements of their remorse about Christian mistreatment of Jews and Judaism. These statements have declared, furthermore, that Christian teaching and preaching can and must be reformed so that they acknowledge God's enduring covenant with the Jewish people and celebrate the contribution of Judaism to world civilization and to Christian faith itself.

We believe these changes merit a thoughtful Jewish response. Speaking only for ourselves—an interdenominational group of Jewish scholars—we believe it is time for Jews to learn about the efforts of Christians to honor Judaism. We believe it is time for Jews to reflect on what Judaism may now say about Christianity. As a first step, we offer eight brief statements about how Jews and Christians may relate to one another.

Jews and Christians worship the same God. Before the rise of Christianity, Jews were the only worshippers of the God of Israel. But Christians also worship the God of Abraham, Isaac, and Jacob; creator of heaven and earth. While Christian worship is not a viable religious choice for Jews, as Jewish theologians we rejoice that, through Christianity, hundreds of millions of people have entered into relationship with the God of Israel.

Jews and Christians seek authority from the same book—the Bible (what Jews call "Tanakh" and Christians call the "Old Testament"). Turning to it for religious orientation, spiritual enrichment, and communal education, we each take away similar lessons: God created and sustains the universe; God established a covenant with the people Israel, God's revealed word guides Israel to a life of righteousness; and God will ultimately redeem Israel and the whole world. Yet, Jews and Christians interpret the Bible differently on many points. Such differences must always be respected.

Christians can respect the claim of the Jewish people upon the land of Israel. The most important event for Jews since the Holocaust has been the reestablishment of a Jewish state in the Promised Land. As members of a biblically based religion, Christians appreciate that Israel was promised—and given—to Jews as the physical center of the covenant between them and God. Many Christians support the State of Israel for reasons far more profound than mere politics. As Jews, we applaud this support. We also recognize that Jewish tradition mandates justice for all non-Jews who reside in a Jewish state.

Jews and Christians accept the moral principles of Torah. Central to the moral principles of Torah is the inalienable sanctity and dignity of every human being. All of us were created in the image of God. This shared moral emphasis can be the basis of an improved relationship between our two communities. It can also be the basis of a powerful witness to all humanity for improving the lives of our fellow human beings and for standing against the immoralities and idolatries that harm and degrade us. Such witness is especially needed after the unprecedented horrors of the past century.

Nazism was not a Christian phenomenon. Without the long history of Christian anti-Judaism and Christian violence against Jews, Nazi ideology could not have taken hold nor could it have been carried out. Too many Christians participated in, or were sympathetic to, Nazi atrocities against Jews. Other Christians did not protest sufficiently against these atrocities.

But Nazism itself was not an inevitable outcome of Christianity. If the Nazi extermination of the Jews had been fully successful, it would have turned its murderous rage more directly to Christians. We recognize with gratitude those Christians who risked or sacrificed their lives to save Jews during the Nazi regime.

With that in mind, we encourage the continuation of recent efforts in Christian theology to repudiate unequivocally contempt of Judaism and the Jewish people. We applaud those Christians who reject this teaching of contempt, and we do not blame them for the sins committed by their ancestors.

The humanly irreconcilable difference between Jews and Christians will not be settled until God redeems the entire world as promised in Scripture. Christians know and serve God through Jesus Christ and the Christian tradition. Jews know and serve God through Torah and the Jewish tradition. That difference will not be settled by one community insisting that it has interpreted Scripture more accurately than the other; nor by exercising political power over the other. Jews can respect Christians' faithfulness to their revelation just as we expect Christians to respect our faithfulness to our revelation. Neither Jew nor Christian should be pressed into affirming the teaching of the other community.

A new relationship between Jews and Christians will not weaken Jewish practice. An improved relationship will not accelerate the cultural and religious assimilation that Jews rightly fear. It will not change traditional Jewish forms of worship, nor increase intermarriage between Jews and non-Jews, nor persuade more Jews to convert to Christianity, nor create a false blending of Judaism and Christianity. We respect Christianity as a faith that originated within Judaism and that still has significant contacts with it. We do not see it as an extension of Judaism. Only if we cherish our own traditions can we pursue this relationship with integrity.

Jews and Christians must work together for justice and peace. Jews and Christians, each in their own way, recognize the unredeemed state of the world as reflected in the persistence of persecution, poverty, and human degradation and misery. Although justice and peace are finally God's, our joint efforts, together with those of other faith communities, will help bring the kingdom of God for which we hope and long. Separately and together, we must work to bring justice and peace to our world. In this enterprise, we are guided by the vision of the prophets of Israel:

It shall come to pass in the end of days that the mountain of the Lord's house shall be established at the top of the mountains and be exalted above the hills, and the nations shall flow unto it . . . and many peoples shall go and say, "Come ye and let us go up to the mountain of the Lord to the house of the God of Jacob and He will teach us of His ways and we will walk in his paths." [Isaiah 2:2–3.]

Tikva Frymer-Kensky, University of Chicago
David Novak, University of Toronto
Peter Ochs, University of Virginia
Michael Signer, University of Notre Dame

About the Author

In my *Vision of Love,* I mention how often I've been put into challenging situations—an unending series of threats, dangers, and trouble, which I endured and survived thanks to incredible luck, coincidences, and rescues. One good thing that issued from these challenging life events is that they furnished good materials for this book!

Also, despite all that, I live a great life at age 84 (when I published this book). As I mentioned, *A Vision of Love* is a sort-of sequel to my Holocaust memoir, *I Live in a Chickenhouse,* first printed in 1995, and since translated and republished in Dutch, German, and Hebrew.

My story also resulted in a play of the same title, with which I toured in Switzerland and Germany for a successful theater season (the German version is named *Ich Wohne in Einem Hühnerhaus*) and I have it ready for a run on the American stage.

My story has also appeared as a documentary, "Rediscovering My Childhood," and, most exciting of all, is on its way to providing the plot to a full-length feature film, tentatively titled *The Last Witness.*

As a healthy octogenarian who celebrated his 84th birthday in 2017, people see me as an inspiring father or grandfather figure, full of common sense and appreciation of life. Besides occupying myself with writing books and derivatives, I work on how people my age can contribute to the community and how they can pass on life experience and practical knowledge to the next generation. I share this process in programs at life care centers, community groups, and spas.

My education includes a bachelor's degree in economics from Ohio State University and a master's degree in journalism from the University of Wisconsin. I am married to Helena, née Levine, and have one surviving child, a daughter, Liora, who lives with her husband and children in Switzerland.

www.ingramcontent.com/pod-product-compliance
Lightning Source LLC
Chambersburg PA
CBHW052125270326
41930CB00012B/2767